Wall paper

Published in 2006
by Laurence King Publishing Ltd
4th Floor, 361-373 City Road
London EC1V 1JJ

enquiries@laurenceking.co.uk
www.laurenceking.co.uk

Designed by Rudd Studio
www.ruddstudio.com

Cover images by Colorflage (top) and Persijn Broersen
and Margit Lukács (bottom)
Title page image by Nice
Frontispiece by Antoine et Manuel

A catalogue record for this book is available from the
British Library.

ISBN-13: 978 1 85669 502 2
ISBN-10: 1 85669 502 6

Printed in Hong Kong

Wall
paper

Lachlan Blackley

Laurence King Publishing

Contents

Foreword

The era of white-washed minimalism is very much a thing of the past: the desire to customize space is making a comeback. After a seemingly endless dearth of ornament and romanticism in interior design, the art-like custom prints and landscape pieces which we're seeing today, are a far cry from the repeat-pattern wallflowers of yesteryear.

Wallpaper seems to have come full circle, having originated in the Qin Dynasty of ancient China as landscape-style, hand-painted rice paper - and today once again typified by decorative large-format artworks created by leading contemporary creatives. The new wave of wallcoverings function once more as a main feature rather than as a backdrop, reflecting the shift in interior styling towards 'maximalism', and the merging of art and design.

As communication design is increasingly accepted as a contemporary art-form and its pioneers as creative innovators, we're seeing a whole new set of skills and tools emerge that are transforming the interior landscape. Meanwhile, graphic design, interior design, art and architecture are merging together making labels redundant. As a result of these developments, the standard-setting contemporary creatives use both traditional analog and the latest digital tools, creating limitless new approaches to spatial experience.

The boldly decorative, boundary-breaking designs featured in this book indicate a demand for interior styling which expresses individuality after the identikit, bare-walled minimalism of the 1980s and 1990s. This growing demand for strong, dynamic statements is giving way to new perceptions in interior styling. At the same time our understanding of art and design - and their function in society - are transforming. Using the wall as their palate, contemporary creatives are making wallscapes that will define the room, rather than merely adding to it.

—Max Akkerman and Lotje Sodderland

Maxalot was formed in Barcelona in 2003 by Max Akkerman and Lotje Sodderland as a way of bringing together 'graphic design, iconography, street art and all the hybrids in between to create exhibitions and creative projects', and now incorporates a gallery, boutique and website. Exposif wallpapers have been developed in collaboration with leading names in graphic design, photography and illustration and reflect a shift in interior styling that uses wallpaper as both art and decoration. In collaboration with EPSON Maxalot offers high quality, luxurious wallpapers to custom order, marrying outstanding design with new developments in print technology.

Introduction

Wallpaper is back. No longer bland peripheral decoration, wallpaper today shouts out individuality. It is customized to enhance our homes, commercial spaces – bars, restaurants and hotel interiors, and installed as art in museums and galleries.

After the stark minimalism of the 1990s, the revival of ornament has been a significant factor in the re-emergence of wallpaper. A millennium-induced urge for complex décor, dubbed the 'decriminalization of ornament', has enabled decoration in its many forms to boldly re-enter visual culture. Championed by graphic designers, artists and illustrators, a more Baroque, pattern-rich styling and decorative detail has made its mark again. But this time there is a greater freedom and an element of fun. Art and design have merged and all the rules are thrown out.
No longer confined by floor-to-ceiling wall coverage, artists and designers are enjoying the medium of wallpaper, playing with scale and using the wall as canvas.

Today, visual culture is cross-disciplinary. Graphic designers, artists, illustrators, photographers, fashion and industrial/product designers are all trying their hand at creating wallpapers, blurring the division between art and interior decoration often with startling results. Wallpaper has moved far beyond the simple repeat pattern, and when once wallpapers were created anonymously by designers for large commercial manufacturers, today we see individual artists producing their work as limited editions, as bespoke papers, or in collaboration with manufacturers who are aware that the market has very much changed.

Wallpaper is no longer limited to the traditional paper roll, so the more inclusive term 'wallcovering' is now widely used. Vinyl adhesives, stickers (decals), 3D, animated and even interactive wallpapers express bold new directions, a willingness to avoid definition and of course the rapid advance and use of technology and materials.

Computers are crucial to the development of work that uses decoration in a significant way, and allows greater complexity of design. The recent advances in 'digital craft' and in large-format printing technologies have meant that designers have the scope and freedom to produce work that is as large and complex as they want. This is particularly evident, for example, in the huge works of the artist Peter Kogler, the intense hand-drawn illustrations of Persijn Broersen and Margit Lukács and the landscape papers produced for Maxalot's Exposif collection.

Andy Warhol was the first artist to make a connection between art and domestic products. His well-known *Cow* wallpaper (1966) set a precedent that has been followed ever since and visual artists are now attracted to wallpaper as a medium in part because it can completely envelop a space. Francesco Simeti, Virgil Marti and Assume Vivid Astro Focus use the medium as installations to portray often subversive, socio-political commentary in their work, examining issues such as sexuality, war, human rights and the environment. Along with the dystopian inclusion of dark and ironic themes that is in many ways particular to our time, there is also humour, a playfulness within multiple narratives and ironic reference to history and previous design periods in much of the wallpapers produced today by artists, designers and illustrators.

Fashion has always been closely linked to interiors, and textiles have provided an endless source of design ideas that can be translated into wallpaper. In the past, changing fashions in woven and printed fabrics such as silk brocades, worsteds, block-printed chintz and cotton were echoed in wallpapers. Today, contemporary fashion designers such as Basso & Brooke and Eley Kishimoto are extending illustration and beautiful fabric prints from the catwalk to the wall, while fashion photographer Rachel de Joode cleverly renders images of her models into repeat pattern.

Many designer-makers creating wallpaper today combine traditional handcraft techniques and printing with the latest technology, computer-aided imagery and photography. Drawing on nature and retro sources of inspiration, designers such as Rachel Kelly, Tracy Kendall and Lisa Stickley are producing commercial papers that are interactive, textural and bold design statements, which are not necessarily meant to blend in with the carpet. These designers continue to push the boundaries of craft technique and application.

Perhaps the greatest advance is interactive wallpapers: solar-powered, UV-sensitive, noise reactive wallcoverings; papers imbedded with electroluminescent materials; and interactive paper that works like a display, giving you the possibility to change patterns and content as you wish (or even read email on the wall). Christopher Pearson's innovative reworking of a William Morris paper animates willow leaves on an LCD panel and is an exciting example of how technology is being used to expand the definition.

Wallpaper design has been refreshed. The dynamic and extremely beautiful work in this book is a small cross-section of the various directions artists and designers are taking with their compulsion to decorate the wall. Free of the previous century's technical constraints but still inspired by the past, there seem to be endless possibilities with 'wallpaper' and it will be interesting to see how it continues to evolve.

Acknowledgments
My thanks and appreciation to the following, whose kind support and contribution have helped make this book possible: Wolfgang Matt, Montse, Helen Evans at Laurence King Publishing, Ellie Ridsdale at Rudd Studio, Mark Valli, Lee Williams, Julia Schatz, Markus Strasser, and Max and Lotje at Maxalot.

Lachlan Blackley is a design writer and editor. He is the former features editor at *Graphic* magazine and the co-editor of *Graphic 08: Ornate!*

Absolute Zero Degrees

Keith Stephenson is founder and head of design at London-based design studio, Absolute Zero Degrees. Pattern and decoration play a big part in their design solutions for both independent and corporate clients.

Absolute Zero Degrees has its own range of wallpaper – *Bees*, *Swallows* and *Dandelions*, designed and produced between 2004 and 2006, exclusively for Places and Spaces, London. One of the prints, *Swallows*, was short-listed for *Elle Decoration*'s Future Classics Awards, 2005, and has appeared in numerous magazines and on television. *Dandelions* launched recently in New York as part of an exhibition, 'The British Influence'. The New work *Deer* is designed by and for Absolute Zero Degrees.

Opposite: *Bees*
Left: *Swallows*
Above: *Deer*

Photography: Ian Rippington,
John Warren and Keith Stephenson

What would you say are the main influences on your work or style? Where do you draw inspiration?
The main influences for *Swallows* (autumn), *Bees* (spring), *Dandelions* (summer) and *Deer* (winter) were nature, optical effects and the work of M.C. Escher. Each print is about seasonal metamorphosis, and has natural objects transforming into others: autumn leaves turn into migrating swallows; honeycombs turn into bees and butterflies; and deer appear from a forest of bare winter trees.

What turns you on as an artist? What do you really like?
Colour and texture turn me on – I love vintage textiles by Lucienne Day, the contemporary textiles of Eley Kishimoto and 1960s Portmeirion crockery designs such as *Magic City*. The past plays a big part in what I do. The thing I find particularly interesting is the way each era reinterprets styles and influences from a previous time – like the 1960s take on Victoriana, the 1970s over-lush interpretation of art nouveau or this decade's view of the 1980s.

Are there certain things you consider when designing a paper?
Could I live with it in my environment? Ultimately you are designing for yourself and if you can't live with it – then who can? Because our wallpapers are independently produced, the quantities are lower, which has a direct influence on unit price, so production cost limitations are something to keep in mind, such as the number of colours we can work in per design.

What's your preferred method of production and materials?
The wallpaper is printed on 80-year-old machinery by print technicians with a high level of craftsmanship who blend the colours by eye, using china clay added to the colour. This gives them a rich texture. A natural degree of movement in the roller means that the end result has a unique, hand-printed quality.

What do you most dislike?
Being pigeon-holed. Our work covers brand identity design, retail spaces, print and publishing, and there are many other multi-disciplined design teams around – such as Doshi Levien – so it seems quite old-fashioned to expect designers to stick to delivering one thing.

What's the future of wallpaper? How do you see it evolving?
I imagine wallpaper will do what it has always done – go in and out of 'high fashion' while remaining the mainstay of the traditional decorator's world. I think the cutting-edge of wallpaper has the potential to become even more innovative – experimenting with a mixture of light, lenticular effects and new developments in digital technology – such as the impending 3D printing capabilities.

Left: *Deer*

keith@absolutezerodegrees.com
www.absolutezerodegrees.com

Birgit Amadori

Birgit Amadori was born and raised in Frankfurt, Germany, where she attended the University of Art and graduated in 2002 with a degree in visual communication. Her main focus has always been illustration and she has continued a career in this field since graduating. Birgit has lived and worked in Los Angeles since 2004. Most of her clients are part of the entertainment industry in LA, but she also works for various clients internationally including Lufthansa, Virgin Atlantic, Volkswagen, Suzuki, Montblanc, Shift Japan and Die Gestalten Verlag. She has won several awards in illustration competitions for US-based magazines (*Step Inside Design, HOW Magazine)* and associations (Society of Illustrators, American Illustrators). She considers illustration her job as well as her hobby and does not do much else besides drawing in her free time.

'I was one of 20 participating artists from all over the world for "Hotel Fox", a project sponsored by Volkswagen to promote their new model of "VW Fox" conducted by Die Gestalten Verlag, Germany in 2005. I designed the interior of three hotel rooms as well as carpets and wall designs in the hallways. I am currently very interested in myths, legends and mystical symbols like the tarot deck etc. and I wanted to design magical rooms (in the traditional sense). The two main concepts *King's Court* and *King's Forest* both contain images of the fox, traditionally known as the traveller between worlds, the maker of the northern lights, the shape-shifter or simply the shrewd hunter who roams the woods at night. I built the rest of the contents around this image and came up with something fairytale-ish and magical.'

King's Forest (Room 217): 'you are invited to spend the night at *King's Forest*. The forest is populated with beings beyond your imagination but the fox will be there to guide you. *King's Forest* is a place of spiritual freedom, and also a place to gather energy, because red is the colour of the fox, the colour of energy, passion and courage. Take a stroll through *King's Forest*; see what secrets are hidden behind its trees.'

Right: *King's Forest* (Room 217)

Opposite and right: *King's Court*
(Rooms 509 and 510)
Photography:
www.diephotodesigner.de

birgitamadori@gmail.com
www.amadori.org
www.hotelfox.dk

What would you say are the main influences on your work or style? Where do you draw inspiration?
Growing up I loved (and still do) art nouveau. Nowadays I draw inspiration from my surroundings: music, movies, dreams … other people's portfolios (just kidding).

What inspired you to work with wallpaper? What is it you like about this medium?
I'm in love with patterns. For my illustrations, I create custom-made patterns that I use on clothes etc. that my characters wear. I'd love to make my own wallpapers and make really nice patterns for them.

Are there certain things you consider when designing a paper?
The pattern should not give you motion-sickness when you put it on the walls of your room.

To repeat, or not repeat?
Wash, rinse, repeat.

Less is more? Or blast the place with colour and pattern?
Blast it, I say.

King's Court (Rooms 509 and 510): 'the king and queen have gathered their magicians, jesters, counsellors, fortune-tellers and other mystical court members to greet you. Blue represents the *King's Court* and is associated with trust, loyalty and honesty. Also it is the colour of the sky and the deep sea, which suggest infinite freedom. *King's Court* is designed to soothe thoughts, a place to ponder over decisions from different points of view. The various characters represent multiple ways of approach – daring, defensive, seductive, curious, secretive, optimistic, mystical … Be the king's honoured guest and let his court members inspire you.'

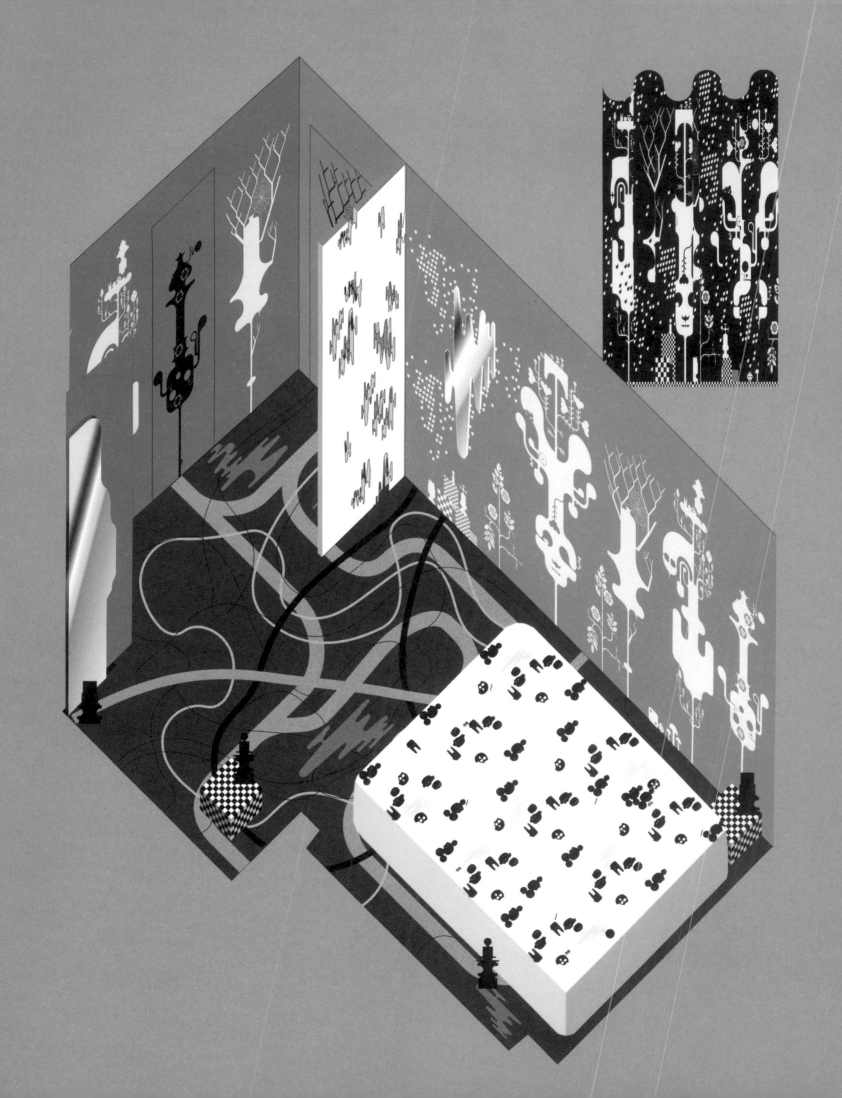

Antoine et Manuel

Associates since 1993, graphic designers and art directors Antoine Audiau and Manuel Warosz work mainly in the spheres of culture and fashion. They each explore their favourite fields and creative methods, resulting in output, which, though diverse, has an obvious unity. Moving from dance to fashion via contemporary art and design, the duo has defined a singular graphic style. They have designed graphic identities for Christian Lacroix, the Collection Lambert in Avignon, season posters for choreographic centres (Centre National de Danse Contemporaine d'Angers) and theatres (Comédie de Clermont-Ferrand Scène Nationale) and displays (Galeries Lafayette Paris, Habitat). Their next projects will lead them to an ever greater involvement in design for the home.

These images are from Room 209, *Chance*, Hotel Fox, Copenhagen, Denmark. The vinyl transfers used are also from the *Forêt* collection, a project initially undertaken for Habitat, comprising ten tiles (50 x 50 cm each) that you combine together, allowing an infinity of compositions.

'I'm in a forest. I feel comfortable. On the walls, a poetic forest appears. Every single element of the room, objects, curtains, furniture, tell me a story about Spirits of the Forest. I'm walking through. I am a small animal searching my way. Am I going right or up, left or down? Trees are like chess pieces. Rocks are dice. Life is all CHANCE.'

Opposite, above and right: *Chance*

Artists/designers/people you admire most?
Architect Louis Kahn.

What turns you on as artists? What do you really like?
Gardens.

What inspired you to work with wallpaper?
Fairy tales, mythology.

Are there certain things you consider when designing a paper?
Hypnotizing.

What do you always notice or look for when you enter a space?
Artificial light.

Less is more? Or blast the place with colour and pattern?
No rules. But obviously, less isn't an issue for us.

For you, is wallpaper art or décor, or both?
I think it is changing nowadays; it can be both. But actually, I don't want to define art.

What's the future of wallpaper? How do you see it evolving?
Moving wallpapers.

Favourite music to design/work with?
Madame Hollywood (Felix Da Housecat and Tiga's Mister Hollywood version).

www.antoinetmanuel.com
www.hotelfox.dk

Right: *Forêt*, wall transfers kit, Habitat (2004)

Assume Vivid Astro Focus (AVAF)

Rio-born artist Eli Sudbrack founded the creative collective Assume Vivid Astro Focus (AVAF) in New York 2001. As one of the AVAF artists, he is also the group's curator and producer, handpicking his collaborators and choosing other artists' work to show within the pieces. The group works around the world creating wall-size installations and wallpapers, erotic prints, videos, stickers, decals, tattoos and entire interiors that resemble a 1960s animation. The work is the product of an ever-shifting line-up of artists – VJs, DJs, musicians, painters, sculptors, graphic designers, carpenters, tattoo artists – instantly recognizable for its flat colour, visual overload and pop culture references.

AVAF produces wallpapers for specific interiors. Patterns that repeat are avoided and the compositions usually conform to existing or imposed architectural elements. 'I've always thought of architecture and design as necessary knowledge for every person. These practices are ever-present in our lives and even dictate them. People should be able to model space according to their needs and not become part of a gentrified, globalized society that is always trying to flatten us towards one general view, one general behaviour, one Starbucks coffee. Architecture and design are interesting political terrains that are not explored enough; instead they are made expensive and unapproachable.'

'Tom Cruising #1 was part of the MOCA "Ecstasy" installation in LA. The centrepiece was a 9-m plastic sculpture of a naked woman, modelled on Brazilian pornography stars, that stretches across the room into a backbend, arching over a phallic column. The woman has two heads: one male, one female. The faces of Tom Cruise and President Bush are buried in the detailed wallpaper, confetti spills from the giant woman's lips and smoke pours out of a hole in Tom Cruise's mouth in the wallpaper. 'The whole thing will feel somewhere between a fun house and a haunted house, and it's also our way of talking about repression, about Bush trying to pass the amendment to the Constitution outlawing gay marriage, and the new pope planning to ban gay priests.'

Above: *Tom Cruising #1*
Left: *Tom Cruising #2*, installation, Galeria Massimo de Carlo, Milan (2005)

Image courtesy of Peres Projects, Berlin/Los Angeles, John Connelly Presents, New York and Galeria Massimo de Carlo, Milan

Above: *Butch Queen 4.4*

Where do you live and create your work?
We are nomads at this point, living in different cities as we are invited to different projects in different parts of the world.

What would you say are the main influences on your work or style? Where do you draw inspiration?
It varies with time and project – could be German expressionism, a sunny day at the beach, a movie by Fellini, a building by Le Corbusier, a trade fair space designed by Emilio Castiglioni, Memphis, unicorn tapestries, graffiti, William Morris, picture discs, vogue balls in Harlem …

Was there a defining moment when you decided to become a designer?
When I watched *Yellow Submarine* for the first time.

What do you aim to create with your work?
To communicate with other people – to sparkle people's lives with new ideas and gold dust.

What's your preferred method of production and materials?
Regular billboard prints.

What do you always notice or look for when you enter a space?
The existing architecture, the light (natural or artificial), the floor, the way people come in to the space and circulate, the type of walls, the adjacent spaces.

What's the future of wallpaper? How do you see it evolving?
We don't think from a designer point of view and don't think of wallpaper as one element on its own necessarily, but part of a whole environment. We wish people were more and more able to control the spaces they live in, really be more conscious of them, the architecture that involves and how that influences their lives.

Is there something you are most proud of?
Our skate rink project in Central Park, New York as part of the Public Art Fund's 'In the Public Realm'.

Favourite music to design/work with?
Varies according to time and mood. Os Mutantes, Serge Santiago, Cat Power, Kate Bush, Animal Collective, Gal Costa, Peter Lindstrom, Roxy Music, Section 25, Future Bible Heroes, Pink Industry, White Magic, Antony and the Johnsons, Italo Disco, Acid House, Josephine Foster, Kitsune compilations …

Left: *Tom Cruising #2*, installation, Galeria Massimo de Carlo, Milan (2005)

Image courtesy of Peres Projects, Berlin/Los Angeles, John Connelly Presents, New York and Galeria Massimo de Carlo, Milan

www.johnconnellypresents.com

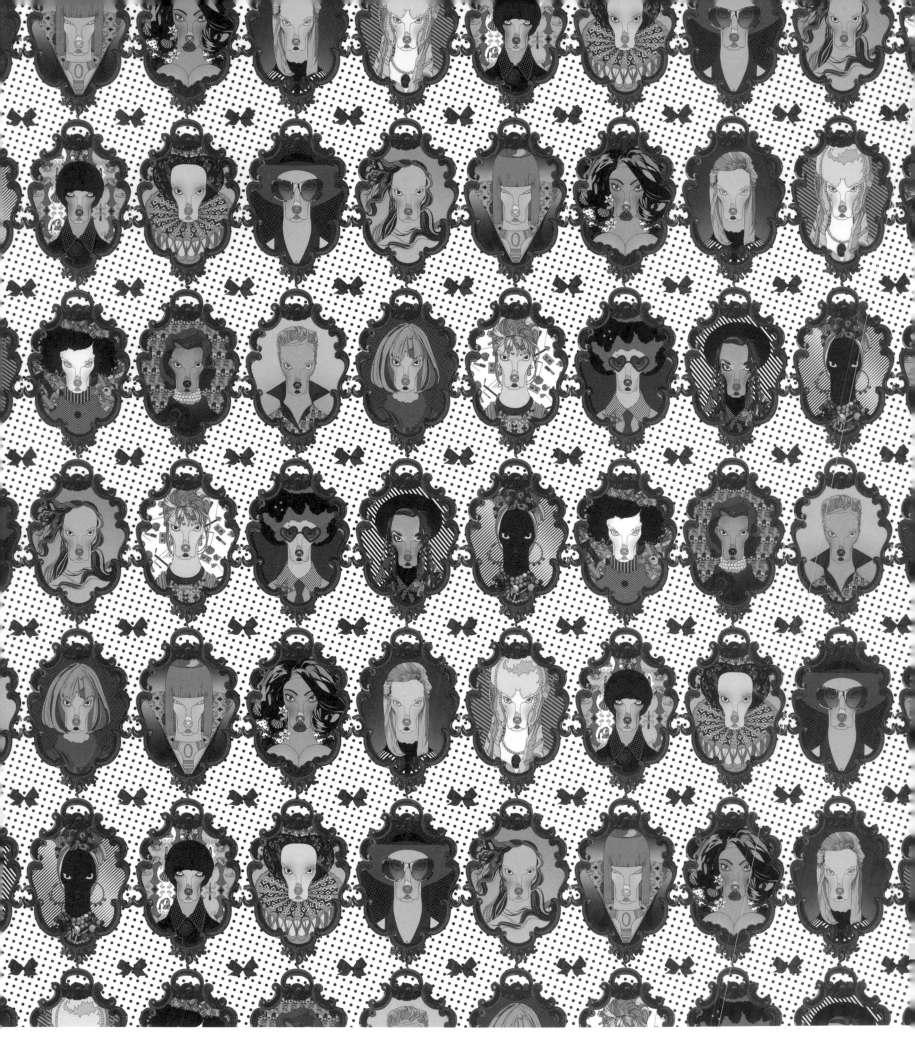

Basso & Brooke

Bruno Basso and Christopher Brooke began working together in 2003 and were catapulted to great heights after winning the London Fashion Fringe competition in 2004. Their style is idiosyncratic, using densely illustrated fabric prints and colourful themes – working in collaboration with a team of illustrators (Alexis Panayiotou and Klaus Schimidt) – to produce work that is fantastic and irreverent. Basso & Brooke continue to exploit digital print to its full advantage, crossing over into interior products such as wallpaper, furniture, ceramics, tiles, carpets and the first-ever printed chandelier (made in partnership with Swarovski for the Crystal Palace exhibition, Milan). They currently sell to 55 stores worldwide, including: L'Eclaireur (Paris & Tokyo), Harrods (London), Maxfield (LA), Harvey Nichols (Dubai & Hong Kong), Tad (Milan), Podium (Moscow) and Wynn (Las Vegas).

'The *Poodles* print is an ironical representation of man's best friend as the ultimate fashion device. It is composed of 16 portraits inspired by icons that have affected our aesthetic perception – Ivana Trump, Boy George, Joan Collins, Marie Antoinette, Carmen Miranda. It was part of the spring/summer 06 collection called *Vanity Affair* and commissioned as a wallpaper by milliner Stephen Jones for his 25th-anniversary exhibition hosted at the Comme des Garçons shop (Dover Street Market) in London 2005. With collaborative illustrations by Alexis Panayiotou.'

Left: *Poodles* wallpaper

Opposite: *Solaris*
Above: *Age of enlightenment*

'The autumn/winter 06 collection *Science & Fiction* is a time-travelling journey of rediscovery, a remembrance of the visionaries and dreamers of the past. The resultant prints are a mix of a romanticized futurism courtesy of authors such as H G Wells and Jules Verne – reinterpreted by a scriptwriter on *The Twilight Zone*. With collaborative illustrations by Alexis Panayiotou and Klaus Schmidt.'

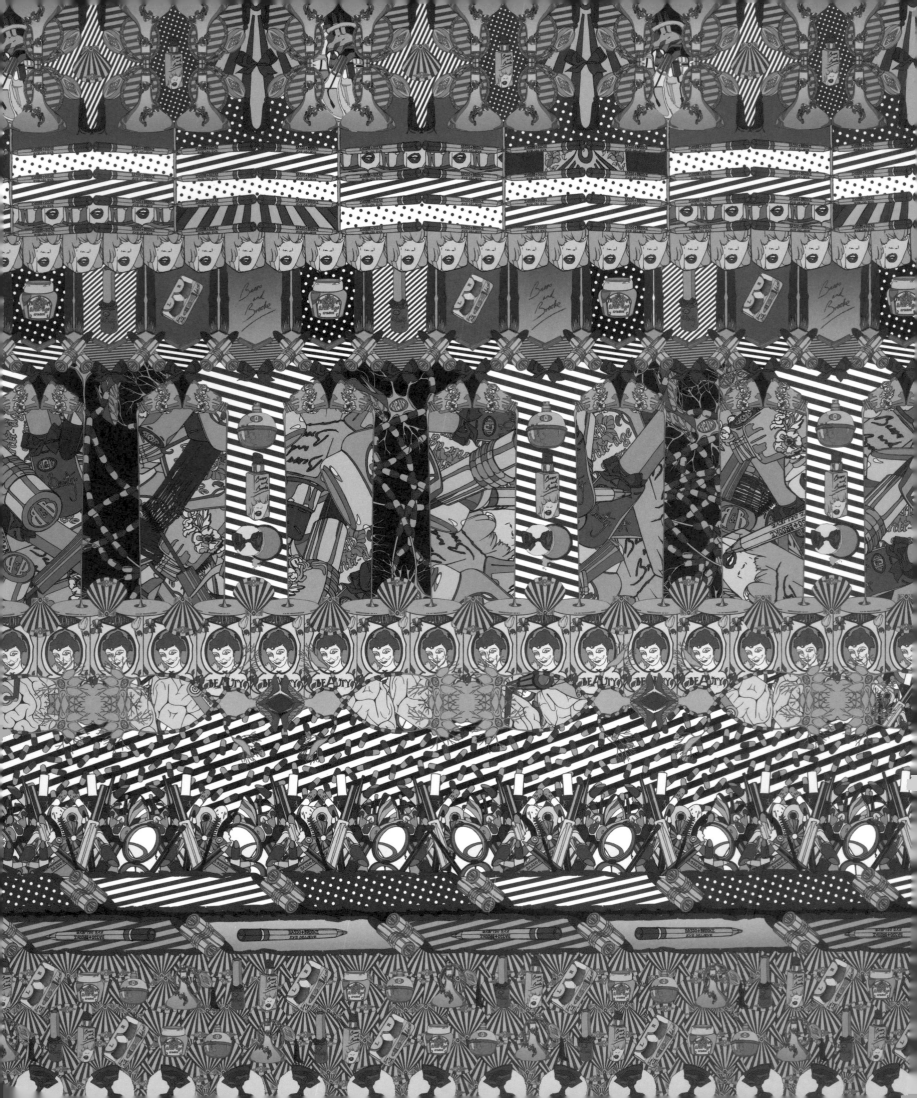

What would you say are the main influences on your work or style? Where do you draw inspiration?
BB – I am interested in the mass-media environment. I like to subvert or change the value of formalities, play with artificiality and frivolities.
CB – We want to slightly confuse people, or at least arouse curiosity. Our work is intelligent and our aim is to provoke discussion. The label is created by two people from very different cultures, which is perhaps its appeal. On first glance the prints can be seen as classic, almost 'Liberty-esque' sometimes, but on further inspection they are an orgiastic carnival of references, and allegories of power.

What do you aim to create with your work?
There is always an intention for our work to be understood not just as an intellectual/conceptual statement, but also an emotional play that will amuse or compete against the stability of your senses. It will provoke a reaction that probably remains from your genetic memory or primitive instincts; it may confuse you in the first moment because there is a misplacement of something or a general idea. It allows you to expect the unexpected, waiting for the stimulation of your curiosity, the strong relation between exhibitionism and voyeurism. It may play ironically and viscerally with archetypes or with commonly found power attributes in our modern society.

Are there certain things you consider when designing a paper?
We design prints for clothes and accessories under the Basso & Brooke label, then they are transformed into wallpaper if the client wants it. We consider so many things, but the most important is to amuse the audience.

What do you always notice or look for when you enter a space?
BB –The smell first, after that, if there are any Fornasseti pieces around.
CB – The exit.

Less is more? Or blast the place with colour and pattern?
More is definitely more.

The whole room, or feature walls?
The whole neighbourhood.

Opposite: *Hollywood*
Left: *Jagger*

bb@bassoandbrooke.com
www.bassoandbrooke.com

Above: *Berlin, Mehringdamm, #1C*

BLESS

Desiree Heiss and Ines Kaag, both born in Germany, met as students in 1993 at the 'concours international des jeunes createurs de la mode' in Paris. They formed BLESS in Berlin in 1996, making their debut with *BLESS N°00* – a collection of rabbit-fur wigs bought by Martin Margiela. Now based in separate cities (Paris and Berlin), BLESS continue to challenge the rules of the fashion industry. Their 'products', which range from clothing and accessories to home interiors, allow multiple, sometimes contradictory, functions and materials to deliver unexpected results – often in collaboration with other designers in clothing, product and graphic design. BLESS have also exhibited internationally, including the Neues Museum in Weimar, Art Metropole in Toronto, Centre Pompidou in Paris, and the Speak For Gallery in Tokyo.

'*BLESS N°29* wallscapes were inspired by and developed for the exhibition "BLESS fits every style" at the Boijmans van Beuningen Museum in Rotterdam. The wallscapes are documents of interiors where BLESS products live or lived and can either be purchased as posters in a 3 x 4 m format (in four, single-metre strips) or as a 'paravent' (screen) made of four wooden panels. These wooden panels include, in addition, three-dimensional shelves that enhance the feeling of confusion as you approach them, where real objects melt virtually into the two-dimensional space. The visitor has the feeling of walking into a collage.'

Top: *Berlin, Mehringdamm, #1A*
Above left: *Car interior, #7*
Above right: *Strausberger Platz, #2C*

Above: *Berlin, Mulackstraße, #5B*

Top: *Berlin, Leipzigerstraße, #3A*
Above: *Bless shop*

Where do you live and create your work?
Ines in Berlin and Desiree in Paris. The work is created in both cities and on our trips abroad.

Artists / designers / people you admire most?
Can be anyone in one specific moment, but no one in particular.

Was there a defining moment when you decided to become designers?
No, we slipped into it as nothing else occurred to be more evident.

What turns you on as artists? What do you really like?
Good food, Aikido.

What do you aim to create with your work?
To fill a gap.

What inspired you to work with wallpaper? What is it you like about this medium?
We developed it for our retrospective exhibition at the Boijmans Museum in Rotterdam (April to July 2006). Since all of our products were made for daily life and not for museums, we photographed some of them in private homes and used these homes as a background to create a more private atmosphere than a museum space can provide.

Do you have an ideal dream project?
To design a car.

What do you always notice or look for when you enter a space?
The first feeling.

What do you most dislike?
Pressure.

To repeat, or not repeat?
What?

Is there something you are most proud of?
Our friendship.

www.bless-service.de

Susan Bradley

After a successful career in the web design industry Susan Bradley returned to education in 3D design, studying furniture design at London Metropolitan University and achieving a first-class honors degree in July 2004. She set up her own business and her designs have won international acclaim, being exhibited in London, Milan and Cologne and featuring in numerous influential design and consumer publications all over the world. Susan recently won the title 'Graduate Designer of the Year' in the prestigious Design and Decoration Awards 2005 and was a finalist in the *Elle Decoration* Design Awards 2005, 'Best Wall-covering' category. In addition to her own product ranges, Susan has undertaken various commissions for both private individuals and commercial clients, in interior and exterior environments including Harvey Nichols, DKNY and George Smith furniture.

'*Outdoor Wallpaper*™ is an innovative new concept that combines traditional imagery with cutting edge technology to create a highly decorative yet functional product – reinterpreting the traditional idea of wallpaper for outdoor spaces, so bringing an element of homeliness and familiarity to the garden. *Outdoor Wallpaper*™ is a highly versatile product that can be used as trellis for climbing plants, screening or simply as a decorative feature or installation creating an immediate impact in any space. Various materials and finishes available include anodized aluminium, stainless steel, powder-coated steel, plywood, acrylic and mirror finish – each giving the product a different feel.'

What would you say are the main influences on your work or style? Where do you draw inspiration?
I love wondering around stately homes and grand old hotels for inspiration, the attention to detail and workmanship is fantastic and very rarely seen today. I recently went to Morocco where it was wonderful to see their gorgeous wooden fretwork and detailed metal lanterns – that really got me thinking – although it was supposed to be a holiday! I am also interested in the technology that is used to create my pieces, and how I can exploit that in different new ways in my design work.

Was there a defining moment when you decided to become a designer?
I had been working in a web design agency, on the project management side of things and one day just realized that I wanted to be on the creative end of things – not just running the projects. The only way to really achieve this was to go back to university and retrain – so I did, and four years later here I am!

What inspired you to work with wallpaper? What is it you like about this medium?
It really happened by accident. I was studying furniture design and my final project was looking at domestic outdoor spaces, and how they can be under used even though they form a large proportion of our overall domestic space. I set out to create designs that would help these spaces feel more familiar and homely, and so hopefully be used more often – so I looked for an iconic domestic furnishing to bring outdoors – and the obvious one was wallpaper. I also wanted the piece to be functional, and not simply decorative.

enquiries@susanbradley.co.uk
www.susanbradley.co.uk

Above: *Japanais design*
Opposite: *Outdoor Wallpaper*™

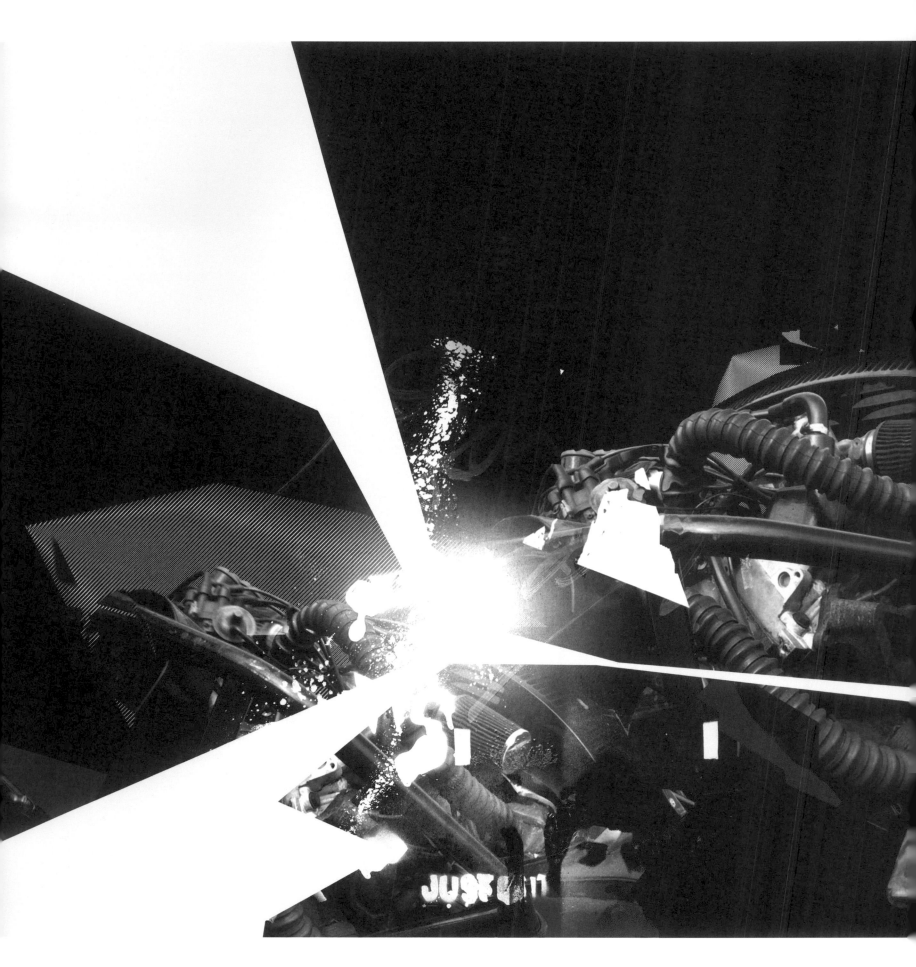

contact@jacksonchang
www.jacksonchang.nl
www.maxalot.com

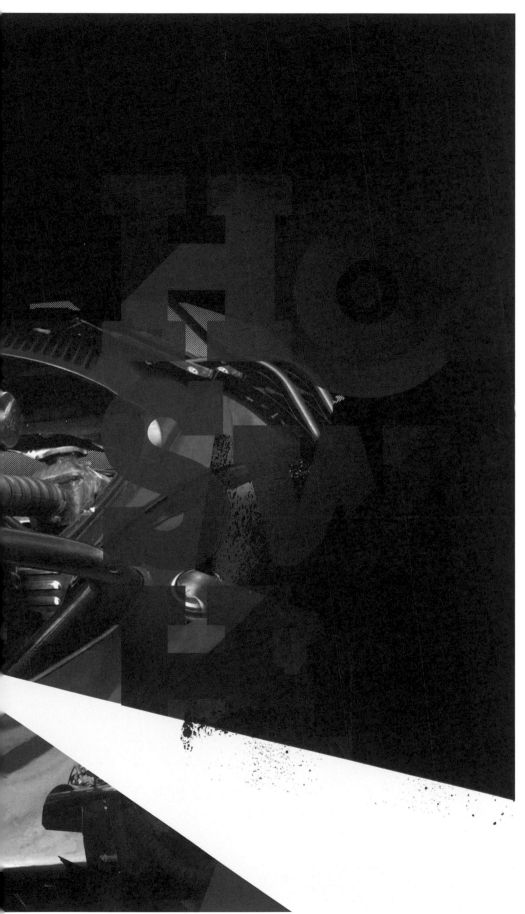

Jackson Chang

Jackson Chang was born in Taipei, Taiwan and graduated cum laude at the Royal Academy of Arts in The Hague, Netherlands. He specializes in progressive graphic design for cultural/dance and youth targeted events. Keen on developing innovative visual codes with his eclectic blend of the corporate and contemporary, his work has strongly contributed to this dynamic scene. Currently working as a freelancer he creates artwork for clients such as Q-dance, Club Silly, Outland, and is setting up a web shop called ibuydesigns. He is also working with renowned fashion photographer/director Denis Piel for Front2End – creating concepts for international marketing campaigns and products that develop brand awareness through innovative use of photography, film, writing and design.

'When I got the opportunity to submit a wallpaper design for Maxalot I jumped at the chance. The other artists involved are some of the greatest of our generation, so I was very excited to be part of it. My submission is not so much a conceptual piece, but rather a visual artwork. Cutting up imagery in this style developed when I was designing for the *BG* magazine (Dutch music and lifestyle magazine) – we needed to find a solution to the fact that the photos delivered for the magazine were either low res or just not interesting enough. So we decided to alter every photo, cut them up and create unique collages for each article throughout the magazine. We did that monthly for about two years, so it's a style that comes naturally for me. I've always been interested in putting a lot of emotion and dynamics into images I create'.

What would you say are the main influences on your work or style? Where do you draw inspiration?
The work that The Designers Republic put out was influential to a whole generation of designers including myself. I guess I'd have to admit that I find most of my inspiration online. There are so many designers/artists showcasing their work online it's almost overwhelming. This is really speeding up the process of development in design on a global level.

Was there a defining moment when you decided to become a designer?
When I was growing up I used to play with Tamiya remote control cars. I was always fascinated with the designs of their boxes, catalogues and labels. The beauty and quality of their design really blew me away. It was then that I started paying attention to the design and typography around me.

What do you aim to create with your work?
I like to create images that trigger some sort of emotional response or bond. I often find myself adding secret messages or metaphors in my work for the train spotters out there.

Above: *Beetlebasher*, Exposif wallpapers, Maxalot

Claude Closky

After obtaining a degree in science, Claude Closky co-founded an art group called the Frères Ripoulin in the mid-1980s. It was subsidized by Agnès B and the magazine *Actuel*. When they split a few years later Claude began to work with language, image and signs. He notoriously published caustic works in the press (*Purple, Selfservice, Libération, Les Inrocks, Ryuko Tsushin* etc.) and created his own media on the internet. He is the author of many books, but also exhibits his drawings, collages, video works and recently conceptual paintings. His works are currently shown in galleries and museums, such as the Centre Pompidou, Paris; the Miró Foundation, Barcelona; the Bass Museum, Miami; and The Ludwig, Cologne. He is represented by the Laurent Godin Gallery, Paris; the Mehdi Chouakri Gallery, Berlin; the Edward Mitterand Gallery, Geneva and the Nicola-Fornello Gallery, Prato.

'One of the major underlying themes of Claude Closky's work is the hyperconsumption of signs through the means of mass consumption, and of advertising imagery in particular. To highlight this he examines just the carriers of the message – the signifiers – and their all-consuming effect on reality, starting from the premise that the realm of representation is so effective that it masks reality and takes its place. In so doing he adopts the reasoning behind advertising and carries it to absurd lengths, stripping the teleology from the messages to leave only their lone statement, amusing, tireless, nauseating, in its infinite forms nothing but an endless repetitive sameness.'

–François Piron

Where do you live and create your work?
Anywhere with an electrical outlet.

What are the main influences on your work or style? Where do you draw inspiration?
In Chinese tea leaves.

Artists/designers/people you admire most?
Andy Warhol.

What do you aim to create with your work?
Pleasure.

What inspired you to work with wallpaper? What is it you like about this medium?
Not patterns.

What do you dislike with a passion?
The telephone.

What would you most like to do?
A somersault.

Above: *NASDAQ* wallpaper
The *NASDAQ* wallpaper was created based on stock exchange results.

Symbol	Price	Change	%	Volume
PTEN	29.03	+ 0.29	+ 0.17 %	429,2
PAYX	19.00	+ 0.03	- 1.30 %	10,722,80
PSFT	18.01	- 0.74	+ 3.76 %	16,144,40
PETM	56.18	+ 1.37	+ 4.20 %	11,348,10
PIXR	37.77	+ 1.44	- 0.12 %	940,80
QLGC	35.7	- 0.01	+ 0.89 %	450,30
QCOM	8.10	+ 0.38		
RFMD	42.85	+ 2.29	+ 5.71 %	6,957,10
ROST	42.39	+ 0.30	+ 7.67 %	8,161,70
RYAAY	4.21	+ 0.05	+ 0.63 %	
SANM	8.00	+ 0.25	+ 0.51 %	479,50
SEBL	49.1	+ 0.122	+ 0.77 %	1,437,90
SIAL	16.02	+ 0.46	+ 2.63 %	2,929,70
SSCC	17.93	- 0.08	- 0.38 %	3,934,00
SPLS	21.12	+ 0.17	+ 5.03 %	53,416,20
SBUX	3.55	+ 1.17	+ 2.74 %	
SUNW	43.85			
SYMC	42.25			
SNPS				
TLAB				

Colorflage

Markus Benesch was born in Munich, Germany, in 1969 and started his own practice at the early age of 17. Since 1989, he has worked as an industrial and interior designer, with a major focus on spaces and products and has his own unique language of design in materials, surfaces and objects. He has collaborated with some of the most important companies in the design sector, such as Abel Laminati, Paul Smith, Essette Leitz, E&Y, Rasch, Neue Modular AG, Mövenpick Group and Messe München. His work has been featured extensively in over 200 publications worldwide. He lectures at L'ESAD (l'Ecole Supérieure d'Art et de Design de Reims), France and at NABA (Nuova Accademia di Belle Arti Milano), Italy.

'Colorflage wallpapers focus on three-dimensional graphics and illusions, ceiling-high colour twirls and fake neon-lamp effects. The special effects can be put in the repetitive lengths at will as the client himself decides on the rhythm of colours and patterns. Aisles, corridors or boring halls can be given a new dynamic. By weaving a pattern between objects and architecture, we create a fused and uniform space. Working with the same pattern for walls and furniture, the furniture blends into the background and appears less visible. Space is being camouflaged by colours, and patterns "colorflaged".'

Opposite: *Weft* wallpaper
Left: *Weft* wallpaper with *Cassetiera Di Alice* plastic laminate chest of drawers.

'*Weft*. The basic principle behind the creation of fabrics is a closed system. Like dreams and experiences, this pattern is endless and holds itself together. Alice's weave is bold, colourful and strong – ready for a life in Wonderland.'

Photography: Benni Könte and Patrick Späth

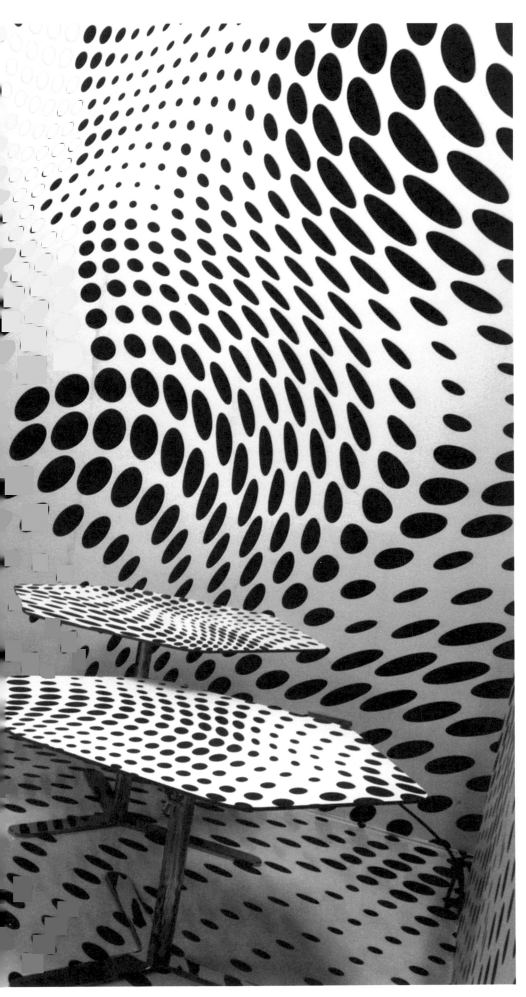

Was there a defining moment when you decided to become a designer?
When I was 9 years old and built my first submarine 'Nautilus' (which unfortunately sank in a fishpond).

What turns you on as an artist? What do you really like?
Good food – Björk, nature, women, music, the Italian cafe in my bar downstairs …

What do you aim to create with your work?
To propose new living scenarios, to change the perception of existing spaces and to add poetry to an environment.

What inspired you to work with wallpaper?
Over the years I have worked with all kinds of surfaces. Wallpaper is the easiest, the fastest and least expensive way to erect new universes.

Are there certain things you consider when designing a paper?
The final space and the people in it, that's what interests me most. I don't care so much about patterns – the space and the people are the most important to me – oops, now it's out!

What's your preferred method of production and materials?
I have no preference, but I insist on finding a new and interesting way to use the production facilities and to take full advantage of the restrictions. Materials are VERY important. I am a fan of materials – I've invented two different ones so far: one for printing and a foam composite.

What do you always notice or look for when you enter a space?
Details, details, details and the general atmosphere.

For you, is wallpaper art or décor, or both?
It's a means of correcting architecture. I think it could be both, but for me it is just a tool, like my laminates, which leads to the quality and effect I want to give to a space.

Is there something you are most proud of?
My sunken submarine and my 5 lb rainbow trout I caught when I was 13. And the first industrially produced wallpaper with a repeat over 6 m.

Left: *Flow Dots* wallpaper
Milan showroom

'*Flow Dots* makes it possible to give a fluid impression to your walls. They no longer appear static or massive.'

Photography: Andreas Pollok

info@markusbeneschcreates.com
www.colorflage.de
www.markusbeneschcreates.com

Rachel de Joode

Rachel de Joode graduated in 2000 at the Rietveld Art Academy in Amsterdam. She mainly works as a fashion photographer and also works in autonomous photography and styling. In her work she aims to show more than the common 'Strike a pose' fashion shoot, using the collective memory of her generation and finding inspiration in everyday life. She makes her models act like they're in a surrealistic, absurd play without neglecting the glamour and symbolism of fashion photography.

'The *Noir Collection*, a range of wallpaper designs, was inspired by dreams and working with topics such as absurdism, decadence and drama. I started producing wallpapers spawned from the idea of "scaling-up" and patterning some of my selected images into cohesive works that can fill a room. Large range revue dancers, marching soldiers or tarot cards are some of my aesthetic themes'.

Left: *Miss Cachecache*
Above: *Miss Picknick*
Overleaf: *Miss White*

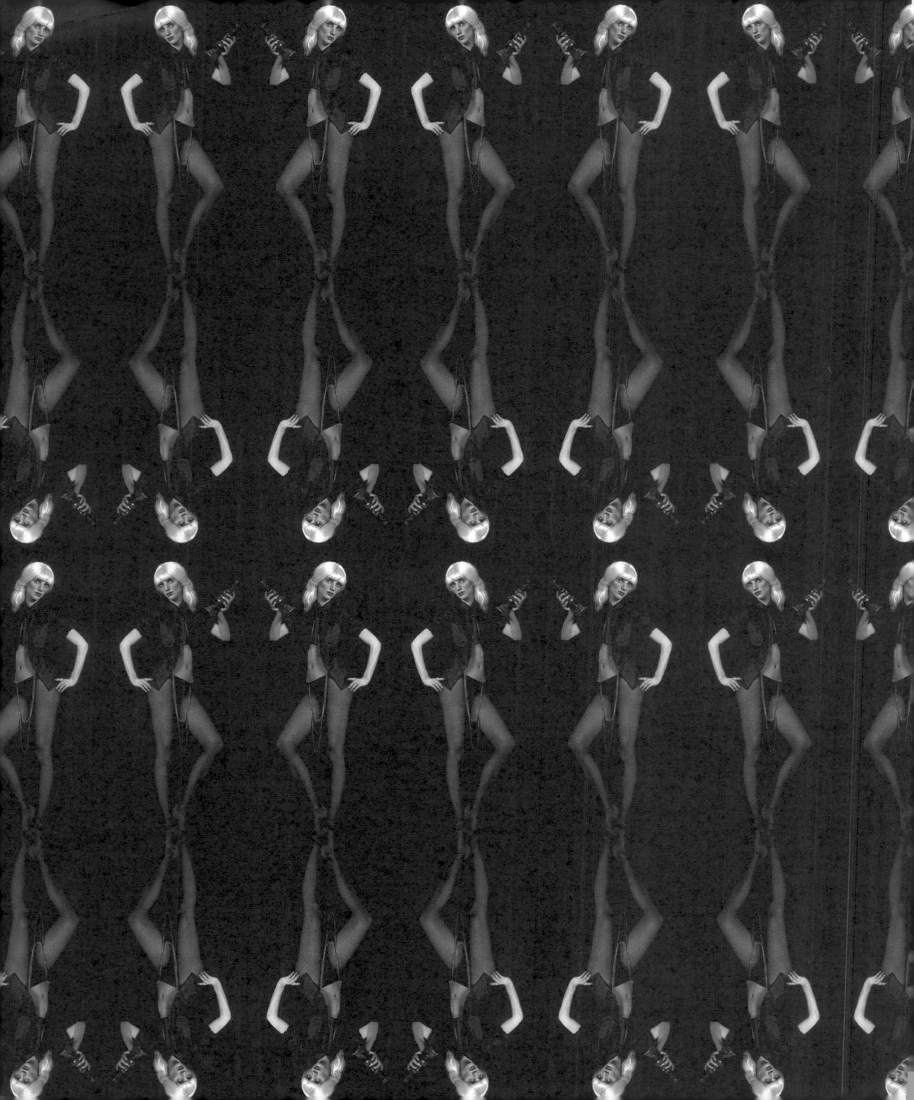

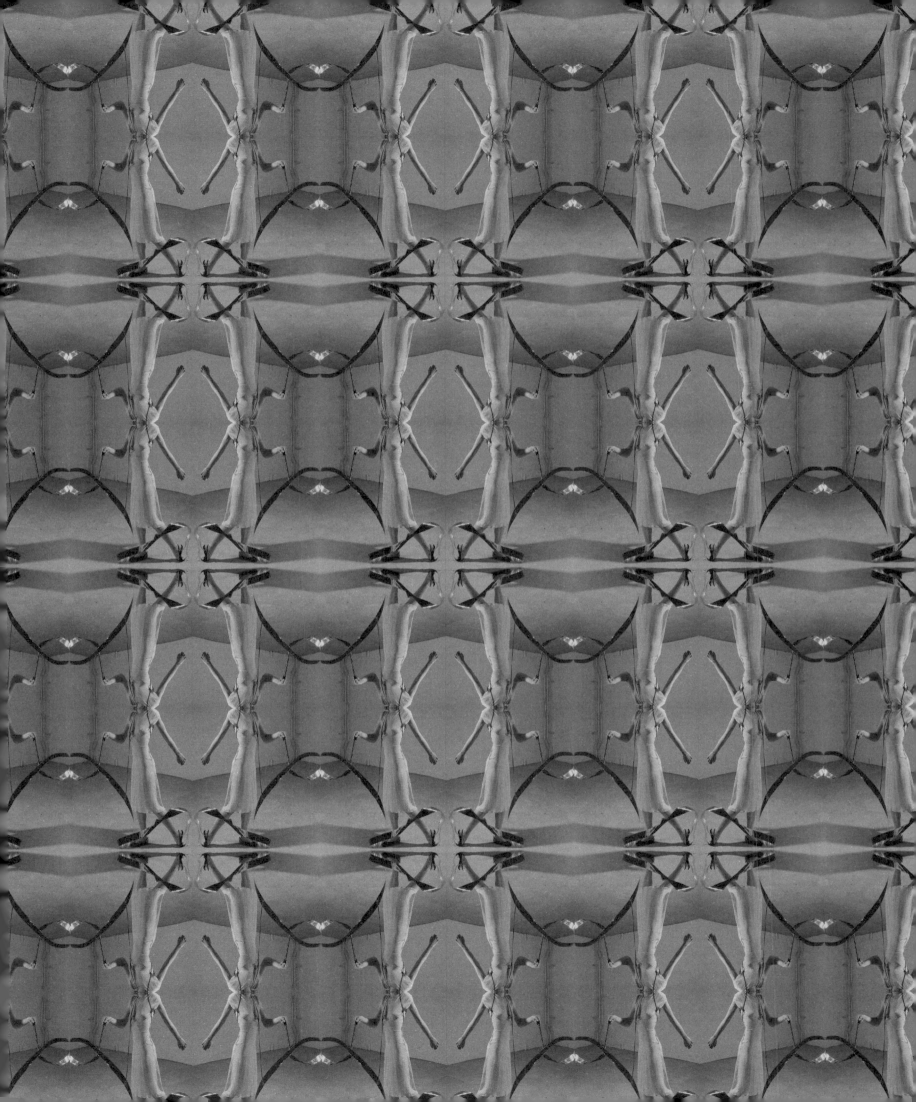

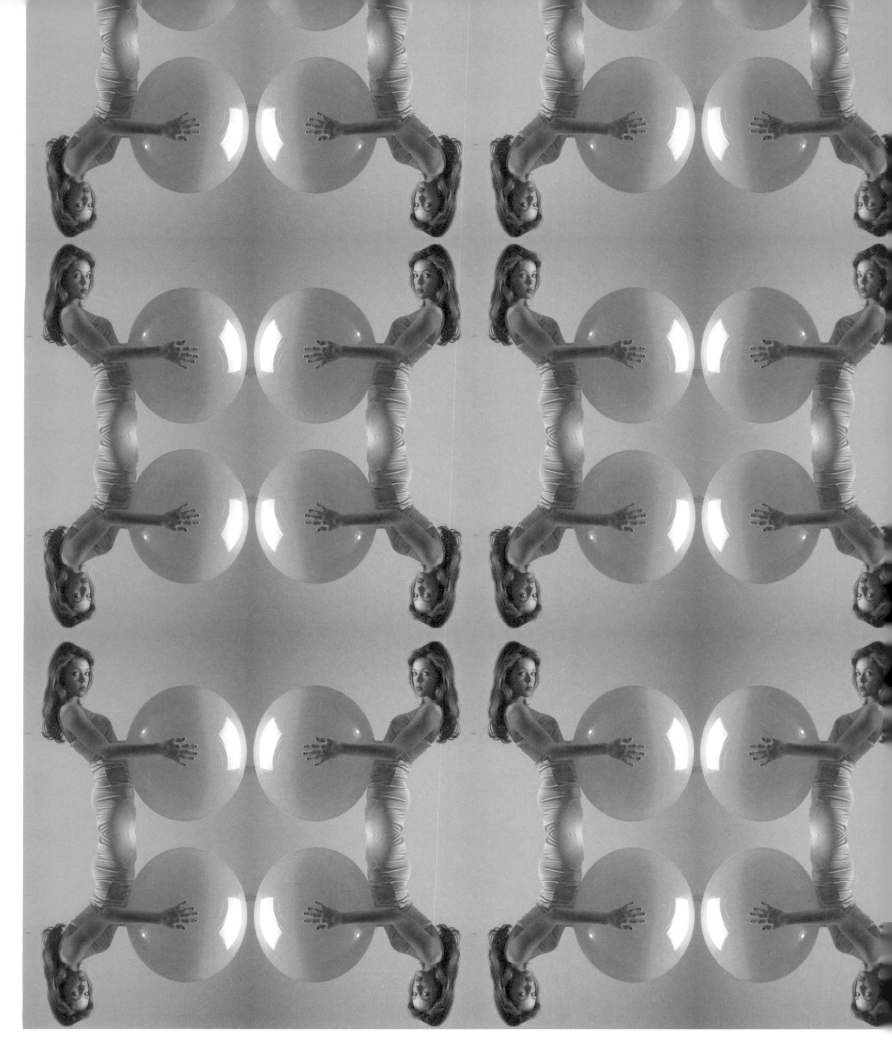

Where do you live and create your work?
Berlin.

Was there a defining moment when you decided to become a designer?
The moment I realized you can earn money with art when you translate it into design.

What turns you on as an artist? What do you really like?
At the moment a special pair of platform YSL shoes and the designs and philosophy of Viktor & Rolf.

What inspired you to work with wallpaper? What is it you like about this medium?
For me the starting point for designing wallpaper was a way to systematically repeat my logo/brand, which is in my case, my photography. Afterwards I discovered wallpaper is a very strong medium because it has such an enormous effect on the atmosphere of a space. I'm very much inspired by historical wallpaper designs, in the charm of baroque and the elegance of *jugendstil* wallpaper.

Do you have an ideal dream project? What would you most like to do?
At the moment it will be to create my own airline company. A special designed aircraft with a customized interior and exterior. Specially cast stewards, stewardesses and pilots in customized outfits.

What do you always notice or look for when you enter a space?
Personal objects, private treasures.

What do you dislike with a passion?
People who can be considered as 'energy suckers'.

Is there something you are most proud of?
My father. And the images I take of my parents.

Favourite music to design/work with?
At the moment it's a top five list of Guns and Roses, Pet Shop Boys, Nirvana, Elton John and New Order.

info@racheldejoode.com
www.racheldejoode.nl
info@soonsalon.com
www.soonsalon.com

Previous: *Rasberry Ribbon*
Left: *Bellabella*

Destroy Rockcity

Originally from the Carolinas, Lee Misenheimer is based in Brooklyn and pursues drawing as well as other creative projects under the guise of Destroy Rockcity. Destroy arose out of post-graduation boredom in the summer of 1994 as a self-published zine of drawings distributed at punky house shows. Lee has shown internationally and contributed to many publications and projects, including *The Drama Mag, Faesthetic, Victionary, Basefield* and Maxalot Exposif Wallpaper Project.

What would you say are the main influences on your work or style? Where do you draw inspiration?
At this point I find myself very inspired by Japanese prints, but I also get a lot of inspiration from my friends ... everyone has their own projects going and we all push each other to be creative and to keep rock'n it out.

What turns you on as an artist? What do you really like?
Drawing is hot.

What's your preferred method of production and materials?
Pencil and paper. I've been playing with tracing paper and vellum lately as well. Then I will bust out the colour in the computer or redraw in Adobe Illustrator if I need it to be vector.

What do you always notice or look for when you enter a space?
When I think about it, I usually look to see if there's some interesting art work.

What do you dislike with a passion?
Negativity.

The whole room, or feature walls?
Feature walls ... no need to overwhelm.

What's the future of wallpaper? How do you see it evolving?
The Exposif Project was really eye opening for me and for my friends. We are stoked on the idea of making art really part of a room or space. I think more people will get into making their own paper whether through the explosion in silk-screening or through access to large format printing with archival inks and interesting paper types.

Favourite music to design/work with?
You can't go wrong with a little Yes, but if you need to rock some shit out ... Bad Brains.

Above: *Current*

me@destroyrockcity.com
www.destroyrockcity.com
www.maxalot.com

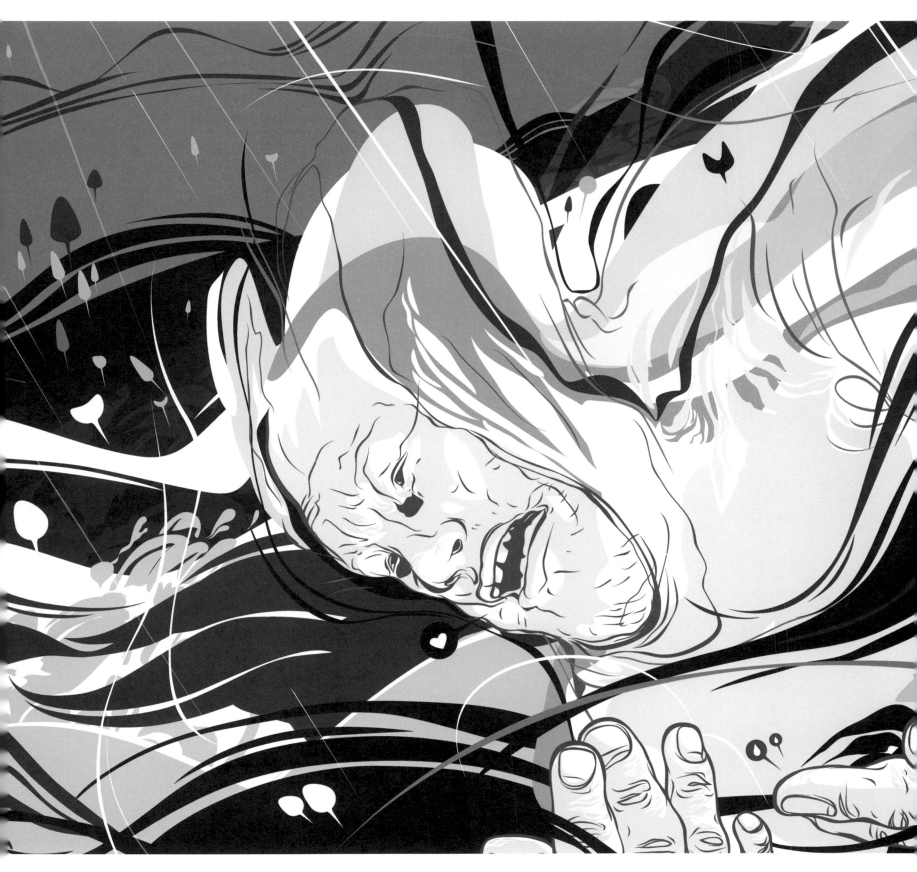

'The title of this work is *Current*. It was part of the Maxalot Exposif Wallpaper Project. I've always liked the idea of creating mini-narratives or mythologies as I work on a piece. I find myself very interested in Japanese mythology lately. Maybe this image shows a mythological figure caught up in a storm or struggle of some sort, or just a man battling his demons. The small creature in the top left of the image is based on my dog.'

Deuce Design

Bruce Slorach was born in 1962 in Melbourne, Australia, and studied fine art at the Victorian College of the Arts. He has enjoyed an extensive career in both graphic design and the arts, beginning in the early 1980s with the design and fabric studio, Abyss Studios. He was also creative director at Mambo Graphics from 1995 until Deuce Design was established in 1999. As director, Bruce is responsible for leading a team of graphic designers who create identities, environmental graphics, print and web design solutions. The studio is responsible for creating some of Sydney's most memorable and creative graphic design work: from customized wallpapers and beautiful fabrics to standalone furniture pieces. Bruce's work has been featured in many well-recognized Australian and international magazines and newspapers, and he has participated in numerous exhibitions over the past 20 years, many of which are permanent acquisitions: the Victoria and Albert Museum, London; the Powerhouse Museum, Sydney; the National Gallery of Australia, Canberra and the National Gallery of Victoria, Melbourne.

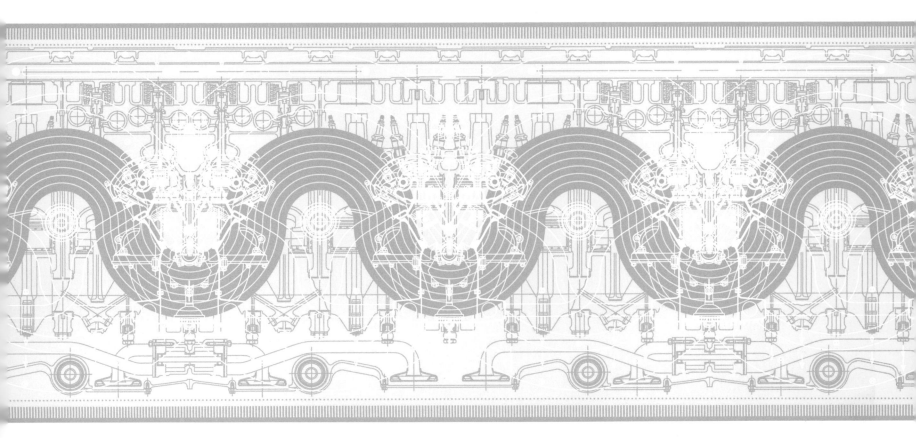

Opposite and above:
Psychedelic Engine, Tow Bar, Surry Hills, Australia (2001)
Photography: Dean Wilmot

'The *Psychedelic Engine* wallpaper was designed for an exclusive cocktail bar cum car showroom. The pattern is an exploded technical drawing of a car engine superimposed over a slot-car track – the serious meets the absurd. It is 1,200 mm x 12,000 mm hand screen-printed silver Mylar print, mounted in a stainless steel frame.'

'Planes, Trains and Automobiles is located in a pub adjacent to a busy train station, hence the "Pop Transport" theme. The customized Mylar wallpaper is a combination/repeat pattern of transport pictograms and iconography interspersed with absurd elements such as skull and cross-bones, wine glasses, people and buildings. The overall effect is dynamic and humorous and the project extends to light boxes, printed Laminex and a router-cut ceiling pattern.'

What would you say are the main influences on your work or style? Where do you draw inspiration?
Anything Japanese, Takashi Murakami, Hardy Blechman, Syd Mead, Tadanori Yokoo, Gordon Andrews, Pierre Paulin, the history of pop culture, William Morris, The Hairy Who, Tex Avery, Piero Fornasetti, Joe Colombo, Memphis, the list goes on ...

Was there a defining moment when you decided to become a designer?
When I was 13 I won the Australian Wool Board agriculture show poster competition; it was a defining moment.

What inspired you to work with wallpaper? What is it you like about this medium?
It was a logical progression; following years of fashion and textile design, it seemed like the next stage, from dressing people to rooms. I love the permanency of wallpaper, as opposed to the seasonality of fashion.

Preferred method of production and materials?
Screen-printing with special papers like Mylar.

What do you dislike with a passion?
Bad repeat patterns, no passion, fence sitters and crimes against humanity.

Less is more? Or blast the place with colour and pattern?
Blast the place with colour and pattern and send them to the moon.

The whole room, or feature walls?
Go the whole hog.

What's the future of wallpaper? How do you see it evolving?
With the development of digital media and large format printing wallpaper has a huge future, the sky's the limit.

How would you like your own work to develop?
More large-scale environmental work where I have the chance to affect people's daily experience.

Opposite and above:
Planes, Trains and Automobiles,
Central Hotel, Blacktown, Australia
(2005) Andrew Moffitt contributed
to Planes/Trains/Automobiles
Photography: Dean Wilmot

design@deucedesign.com.au
www.deucedesign.com.au

Linda Florence

Based in London, Linda Florence creates wallpapers and interior textiles. Past commissions have included homes in Primrose Hill, Ted Baker in Selfridges, London and stores in Dallas, Texas and Orange County, California. Linda Florence graduated from Central Saint Martins, London with an MA (distinction) in design for textile futures. She previously graduated from Duncan of Jordanstone with a first class honours degree in design and won a New Design of the Year award resulting in an exhibition at Index in Dubai, UAE. She has also exhibited her *Morphic Damask* wallpaper in the V&A 'Touch Me' exhibition, 2005. She teaches as an associate lecture at Central Saint Martins, and has taught as visiting lecturer at various colleges and universities in the UK.

'*Morphic Damask* looks at patterns growing in complexity and interest over time. My work looks at surface pattern and texture and challenges where the floor surface starts and ends. I have explored a range of hybrid design concepts such as "wall-to-floor" coverings and temporary surfacing. I have a range of wallpapers that evolve with time and reveal hidden patterns with wear and tear. I create wallpapers with tiles that co-ordinate. Some of the tiles and wallpapers change in pattern the more they are walked on or touched. The work takes inspiration from William Morris and op art. All wallpapers are hand-printed to order.'

Morphic Damask Gold Wallpaper (2005): 'The 3D gold details are hand-cut papers, which are added to the wallpaper after it has been hung. Their positioning is guided by the space the wallpaper is put in, i.e. 3D areas around a window or fire or on the focal point of a wall instead of a painting. This 3D detail I love to make – each one works a little differently as it is handmade and I can build it up in different ways and layers.'

Above, right and opposite:
Morphic Damask Gold Wallpaper

What would you say are the main influences on your work or style? Where do you draw inspiration?
I have always been fascinated by patterns. I collect scraps of materials and love finding new textures and materials. My room is full of artefacts picked up from second-hand shops and handed down to me by my family. My imagery includes traditional Morris, I love drawing in the V&A archives, maze patterns, Bridget Riley paintings and also imagery from my childhood like Space Invaders and Pac Man.

What inspired you to work with wallpaper? What is it you like about this medium?
The varying dimensions are so exciting – you don't run out of space, you just add another strip and you can make grand scales that are viewed from across the room and tiny images that can be explored close up. I have scratchable papers, which were inspired by picking at puffy wallpapers as a child, and wallpapers that have flock and foil on them, mixing textile fibres with matt papers and foil surfaces.

Are there certain things you consider when designing a paper?
I try to mix different scales and unusual colours together. I love working with clients to create a customized colour or pattern combination, making it unique to them and their homes. Some of my papers can have 3D elements added to them once hung, for example hand-cut leathers and felts and papers. The positioning of these can be directed by the architecture of the space around a window or around a fireplace.

Less is more? Or blast the place with colour and pattern?
Pattern. Pattern. Pattern. I love it. It's amazing how patterns can have an impact on you. I can clearly remember the pattern of the 1970s carpet in my parent's home or the covers of my bedding. These things stay with me in my memories of places and events.

Do you have an ideal dream project? What would you most like to do?
I hear China has a large wall!

Opposite: *Morphic Damask Flock*
Left: *V&A Morphic Damask*

linda@lindaflorence.co.uk
www.lindaflorence.co.uk

Linda Florence 61

Front

Swedish designers Sofia Lagerkvist, Charlotte von der Lancken, Anna Lindgren and Katja Sävström completed their masters degree in industrial design at Konstfack and established design group Front in Stockholm 2003. The four like to challenge the basic conventions of product design by exploring radical new ways of interpreting everyday things – extending the range of approaches and in particular investigating the psychological mechanisms behind people's needs, in order to be able to make use of new insights in industrial design.

'Flower Wallpaper is part of the permanent interior design for the entrance to the Tensta Konsthall, an art gallery in Stockholm. In the inner room, silk and plastic flowers are mounted on the wall, like a three-dimensional wallpaper. 'The flowers look so real people asked us what we'd do when the flowers died!'

What turns you on as artists? What do you really like?
Electronics and any kind of advanced technology that we haven't seen before.

What do you aim to create with your work?
We ask ourselves questions about design. We want to explore the possibilities in different fields. Is it possible to create furniture out of an explosion? Who is the designer if we let an animal create the form? A lot of times it is about the processes that are always involved in design and the role of the designer. We do not necessarily have to come up with an answer; the product can be an inspiration to the viewer to ask themselves questions about things.

What inspired you to work with wallpaper? What is it you like about this medium?
We were inspired to work with other dimensions than the 2D graphics that are most common in wallpaper design. The *Flower Wallpaper* is made out of plastic flowers, for instance, to create a three-dimensional wallpaper.

What do you always notice or look for when you enter a space?
Objects that people have in the home – we look for things that tell a story about the people who live there, like memories etc.

Favourite music to design/work with?
Dolly Parton is great to listen to when you're doing your tax return.

Answered by Sofia Lagerkvist.

Opposite, top and above:
Flower Wallpaper, Tensta Konsthall,
Stockholm, Sweden
Photography: Anna Lönnerstam

Left: *Rat Wallpaper*
'We asked animals to help us.
"Sure we'll help you out," they
answered. "Make something nice,"
we told them. And so they did.'
Photography: Anna Lönnerstam

Opposite: *Design by Sunlight*
Photography: Katja K

'*Rat Wallpaper* is part of *Design by Animals,* a series of objects inspired by the habits and habitats of creatures. We wanted to show the designer's role in giving legitimacy to the artistic content of an object. (Will the relationship be different if an animal created the shape – even though the function is the same?) We knew that rats like to gnaw, so we took it from there. We put a roll of wallpaper in the rats' cage and let them gnaw as much as they wanted. When the rats were done chomping through vast bolts of white wallpaper, we were left with a delicate lacy pattern that allowed old paper or paint to show through.

Design by Sunlight is a UV-sensitive wallpaper. The still-life pattern is composed of classic Nordic design objects – a Poul Henningsen lamp, an Ericofon, fresh flowers in a typical Scandinavian vase. The repeated image is UV-sensitive so that when the sun shines, the purplish silhouettes gradually materialize, only to fade again at the day's end. A wallpaper that will never look the same from one day to the next.'

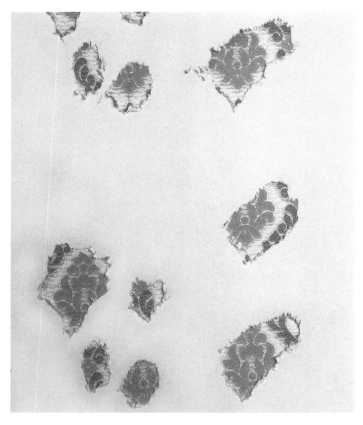

everyone@frontdesign.se
www.frontdesign.se

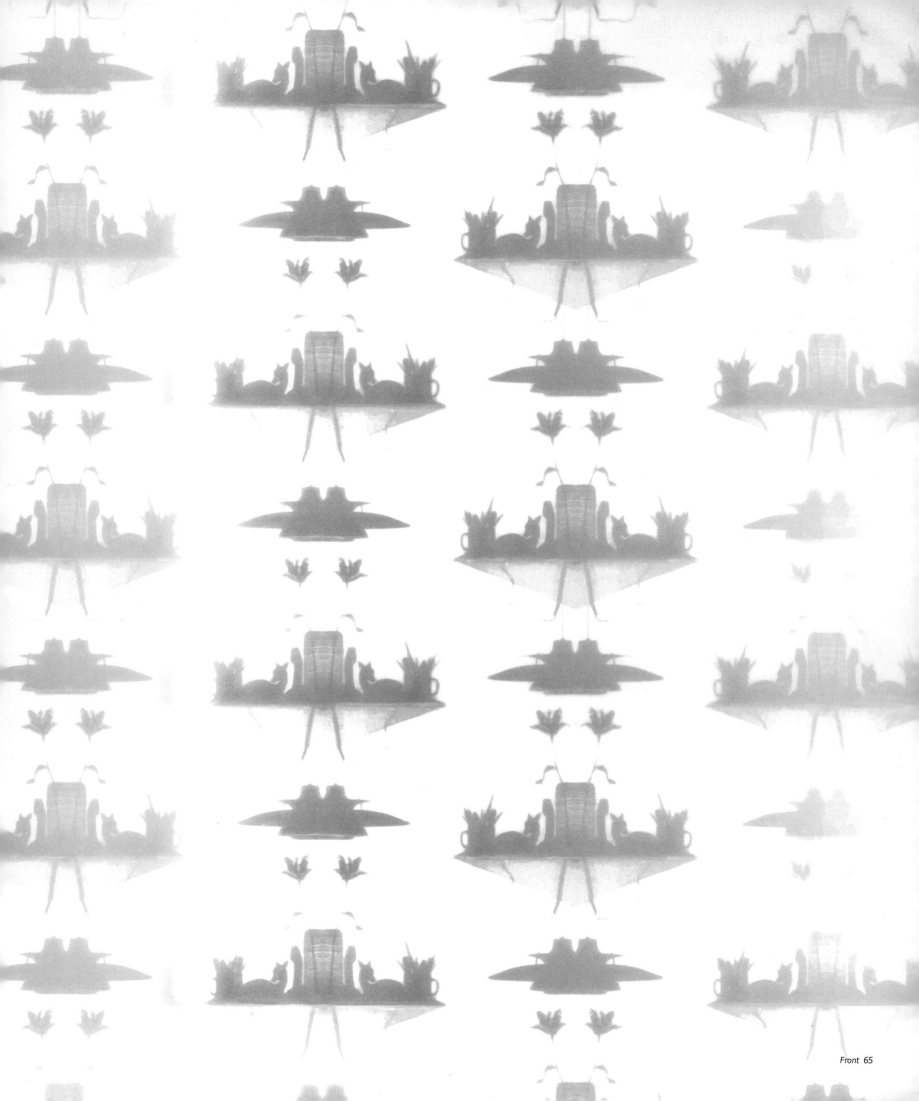

TAKORA Kimiyoshi Futori

Born in Kobe, Japan in 1972, TAKORA Kimiyoshi Futori is a freelance visual creator based in Tokyo. His works cover a broad cultural range and various disciplines within graphic design, including logos, characters, animation and textile design for fashion labels Comme des Garçons Homme and Dresscamp. He has contributed to a number of magazines including *Vision*, *Cream*, *Wired*, *Milk* and *American Illustration* and has also held exhibitions in both Japan and abroad. TAKORA aims to bring a new life and a pop taste to his work within the broad commercial scene. His motto is 'catchy is everything!'.

'*Cheap Pop Fancy Forest* was part of my solo exhibition "Don'tMind". The work covered the Soso Café in Sapporo for a month. I established own my label Don'tMind to produce my products and this piece of work is the first in a series of wallpaper.'

Opposite and above:
Cheap Pop Fancy Forest, Soso Cafe,
Sapporo, Japan
© 2003 grAphic tAkorA + Don'tMind

'*Samurai Garden* was created for the Exposif Wallpaper Project run by Maxalot in Barcelona. The exhibition was held in Europe as well as at Rocket, Tokyo, and at Soso, Sapporo.'

Artists/designers/people you admire most?
To be honest, no one now. Because we have to create our scene and time by ourselves, I admire all my creator friends in the same generation all over the world.

Was there a defining moment when you decided to become a designer?
When I was looking for a job! At that time the Japanese economy was down, so it was really tough to look for the right job. But in another way, it was a big chance to work freelance. Luckily I was a bit crazy about focusing on my future. I didn't feel fear at all.

What do you aim to create with your work?
Make people happy!

Do you have an ideal dream project? What would you most like to do?
I would like to design a surfaced wall on a school building or leisure space. Like a monument for the city or an area people share.

What do you always notice or look for when you enter a space?
Colour! Smell!

What do you most dislike?
Dark colour! It makes me depressed. And a closed mind, because it makes our situation worse to live in! Imagination brings us space to be creative. An open mind can bring us this imagination more than you expect.

Favourite music to design/work with?
All music with pop and soul feeling from all over the world. I love 1960s Japanese cinema music. It is so cheesy! Especially Akira Kobayashi, a funky guy who is a singer and actor.

info@graphictakora.com
www.graphictakora.com

Right: *Samurai Garden*
© 2005 grAphic tAkorA

Rachel Kelly

Rachel Kelly studied surface pattern and printed textile design at Leeds College of Art and Design and graduated from Central Saint Martins College of Art & Design, London in 2001 with an MA in design for textile futures. Rachel established *Interactive Wallpaper™* and has gained critical acclaim for her innovative wallpaper design, winning 'Best Design in Wallcovering' by *Elle Decoration* in 2002 and 'Young Designer of the Year' in the Classic Design Awards 2005. She has created designs for the BBC, the Arts Council of England, Urban Outfitters, Topshop, Oasis, Diageo and Crabtree & Evelyn. Rachel's wallpaper is also held in the collection at the Victoria and Albert Museum and has been exhibited at the Design Museum and Crafts Council in London.

'New Shoes was based on the cult TV programme *Sex and the City*. As a bespoke hand printed paper, the idea was to have a colour way for each character. When I designed *New Shoes* I was thinking about how people often use wallpaper off cuts to line chests of drawers. I envisioned the paper to be a really beautiful drawer liner and had this image in my mind for a long time.

The idea of my stickers and decals, which are applied onto my papers, is that they can be added over time, to re-invigorate the paper.'

Where do you draw inspiration?
When I am inspired, I draw. Most ideas come when I am not paying attention and I am relaxed. I might see something while I am going about my daily life or in a book or at an exhibition.

What turns you on as an artist? What do you really like?
I really like crazy patterns and clashing colours. In my own life and home and even in the way I dress, I don't like things to look perfect. I like the clash. I'm not saying I don't like beautiful things. I just really like the point at which ugly becomes beautiful.

What do you aim to create with your work?
Through my work, I aim to show and share with people the joy of print, pattern and colour. I want to design work that pushes the materials and conventions of wallpaper design. I see wallpaper as art and I love the way that something of beauty can become part of everyday life, part of the wallpaper.

Preferred method of production and materials?
My first choice is screen-printing because you get a really nice flat coating of colour. I work with water-based printing inks, which have a chalky finish to them.

To repeat, or not repeat?
Repeats are great, but they can be quite difficult to get right. It's difficult not to over-dominate with repeat. I like to create space with my papers and that is why there is often so much white space in my designs, some room to breathe.

Above: *stickers*
Opposite: *New Shoes* wallpaper
– *Miranda*

studio@interactivewallpaper.co.uk
www.interactivewallpaper.co.uk

Above: *Love Forest*, Exposif wallpapers, Maxalot

Kinpro (Chisato Shinya)

Chisato Shinya (Kinpro) is an illustrator based in Sapporo, Japan, who creates cute character designs for magazines and television advertisements. She has worked on various projects around the world, including book illustrations for Hans Christian Andersen and *The Illustrated Fairy Tales of the Brothers Grimm* (Die Gestalten Verlag), the Hotel Fox project in Denmark, ChillChilly glasses and coasters in Hong Kong, the Maxalot wallpaper project and more. She also continues personal projects and solo exhibitions as an artist. Her warm and pop character world has been increasing her fan base internationally year after year.

'I was very excited when I was asked to participate in the Maxalot project. I have been very interested in the interior and it was my first time producing a wallpaper. Because the size of the wallpaper is very big, I couldn't completely imagine my work until it was actually printed and exhibited on the wall. Then, I tried to imagine the wallpaper actually going out into the world to a normal family, or in to an office ...'

Above: Victor Zabrockis with *Love Forest* in his 18th-century palace apartment in Barcelona, Spain
Photography: courtesy of Maxalot

'With *Time to Imagine it* and *A Feeling Happy* I tried to produce these works imagining the wallpaper in a family house, such as a children's room or a living room. I would be more than happy if I could unconsciously make a space enjoyable with the wallpapers I made.'

Where do you draw inspiration?
It's nature, especially trees. The city I live in has the obvious change of seasons; spring, summer, fall and winter, so I never get tired of seeing it.

Artists/designers/people you admire most?
Paul Land, Dick Bruna, Alexander Girard and my parents.

What turns you on as an artist? What do you really like?
At the moment, I like the time to spend by myself with my cat the most. And a lot of artists' work inspires me too.

Are there certain things you consider when designing a paper?
There is comfortableness, and the feeling like a game when trying to hide a break between patterns.

What do you dislike with a passion?
I've never thought of this … but if pressed I would say that it's the commercial break between TV shows.

Less is more? Or blast the place with colour and pattern?
The ideal is to get colour and pattern together simply.

What's the future of wallpaper? How do you see it evolving?
I would be happy if the wallpaper is used more in a residence, especially in Japan. I would like everyone to take an interest in it – like the Japanese folding screen and papered sliding door in old Japanese ages.

Favourite music to design/work with?
Kid Loco 'A grand love story'; Radiohead 'Kid A'. There is no music when I concentrate on working.

Previous: *Untitled*, Maxalot and
During the sky and the ground

Opposite: *A Feeling Happy*
Left: *Time to Imagine it*

www.kin-pro.com
www.shift.jp.org
www.maxalot.com

Peter Kogler

Austrian artist Peter Kogler was born in Innsbruck, Tyrol in 1959 and lives in Vienna. Kogler is probably best known for his industrially produced silk-screen prints, including the now-famous ant motif shown at the contemporary art exhibition 'Documenta IX' in Kassel, Germany, and the large tube patterns presented at 'Documenta X'. His emblematic, computer-generated patterns, signs and symbols run across wallpaper and completely cover walls and ceilings in site-specific installations, forming networks and structures that disturb known spatial relationships. In addition to his wallpaper works, he has created large-scale installations consisting of inflatable plastic hoses, Jacquard-woven patterns for textiles (curtains and furniture upholstery) and large-scale video projections.

'In Kogler's symbolic spaces, filled with multifaceted codes, an arc of connection can be traced from the current potential provided by digital information and communication technologies back to Expressionist film-set architecture, which provides an important source for the artist. Kogler filters and concentrates elements from cinema, and combines them with elements from Minimal Art and Pop Art.'

–Silvia Eiblmayr

'The grey illusionary tube shape ... is always open to polyvalent interpretations. It can be seen as a pure pattern, as an organoid construction or architecture, as a metaphor for the complicated system of veins and arteries in our bodies, as an extremely enlarged microscopic view of the convolutions of our brains, or lastly as a visualization of electronic circuits and highly dynamic data distribution highways.'

Foreword to Peter Kogler catalogue – Steven Berg, Silvia Eiblmayr and Noelle Tissier

What would you say are the main influences on your work?
The art context.

What inspired you to work with wallpaper? What is it you like about this medium?
The relation between painting and architecture. The possibility of creating site-specific environments.

Are there certain things you consider when designing a paper?
Architecture and context.

What's your preferred method of production and materials?
Silk-screen and inkjet.

Do you have an ideal dream project?
Set design for a science-fiction movie.

What do you always notice or look for when you enter a space?
The emergency exit.

Right: Installation, 'Documenta X', Kassel (1997). Modular system silk-screen on paper. Photography: © Werner Maschmann

www.peterkogler.net

Above: *Blumen,* electronic wallpaper © Loop.PH Ltd

Loop.pH

Loop.pH is a multi-disciplinary partnership set up in 2003 by Rachel Wingfield with artist Mathias Gmachl – a design and research studio that creates and develops new surfaces and structures, conducts an extensive range of research activities and collaborates with industry. Together they have fabricated reactive surfaces for a variety of environments, from the public to the domestic. Their work aims to provide a more intuitive understanding of our natural environment, from day–night cycles to power consumption. Research into the physiological effects of light and colour on the human body is a strong component in their work. They are developing textile-based ambient displays for the home with active textiles that visualize information through dynamic pattern and colour change. Loop. pH has exhibited internationally with the British Council and at furniture fairs in Milan, Tokyo, Valencia, Stockholm and Moscow. They have shown at the Design Museum and Victoria and Albert Museum, both London, where *Digital Dawn* is now part of the permanent textile collection.

Blumen transforms traditional decorative surfaces into a rich, dynamic display of botanical life. It divides and ornaments space and can be seen in a wallpaper format as sliding panels. By working with traditional pattern-making, Loop.pH have created an ornate printed design, which functions at the same time as a working electrical circuit using electroluminescent technology. The repeating pattern allows the piece to be cut into smaller sections and even reassembled. The *Blumen* print is constructed from a number of addressable cells. Sensing various external stimuli, the pattern emerges and develops in response to its environment. Depending on the space the panels are presented in and the characteristics of the sensors used, an animated pattern language is developed, described in software.

What would you say are the main influences on your work or style? Where do you draw inspiration?
It's quite a typical answer but our inspiration is nature. Nature is a vast source of ideas to mimic and be inspired by, rather than a source of materials to extract, convert then discard. A new design practice can be realized through observing and learning from botanical life, co-operating with it rather than working towards its extermination. Photosynthesis, growth, phylotaxis and response to stimuli can provide a strong framework for 'reactive' surface design.

Above and opposite bottom: *Walltherapy,*
© Loop.PH Ltd

Walltherapy, paint-by-numbers wallpaper (2003), was a collaboration between Rachel Wingfield and Flour aiming to bring together areas of design with neuroscience and colour science. The project was first presented at Designersblock 2003 in London and later at Bury St Edmunds Art Gallery in an exhibition called 'Natural Habitat'. In the exhibition people were invited to contribute and paint on the paint-by-numbers wallpaper after being prescribed a colour from undergoing a short psychophysical test that determines colour preference.

'*Walltherapy* enables everyone to create their own highly individual personal environment from their psychophysically determined colour preferences to suit and possibly enhance people's sense of well-being. It is well established in scientific literature that ambient colour, light and texture can affect mood and behaviour; this is why a conventional decorative surface, such as wallpaper has been chosen as the interface for this experiment.'

What turns you on as artists? What do you really like?
We love botanical life! And use plants in our work as we consider them to be the most sophisticated sensors and displays. We often use technology to try to reintroduce these ideas by creating reactive surfaces inspired by botanical life that reflect and communicate environmental changes.

Do you have an ideal dream project? What would you most like to do?
We dream of creating surfaces that behave as plants do, growing in response to their environment, but essentially to be alive and living.

What do you dislike with a passion?
Waste, over-consumption.

Less is more? Or blast the place with colour and pattern?
We view the domestic sphere as a garden in which we transform traditional decorative surfaces into rich, dynamic displays of botanical life. We believe there is an ancient language of pattern that can be read and understood by everyone. As we believe decoration can become a language I think we are more prone to say 'more'...

Top: *Walltherapy* coloured paint bottles

loop@loop.ph
www.loop.ph

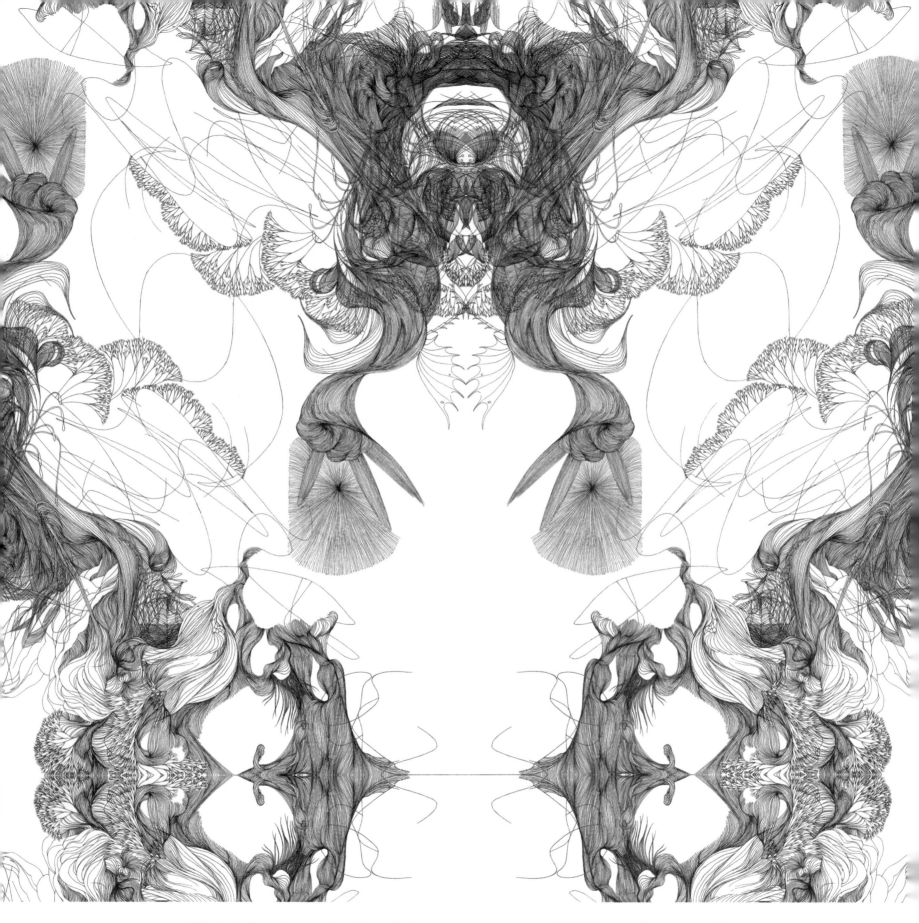

Above: *Volute: Purplepattern*,
Exposif wallpapers, Maxalot

'This is the first time a "volute" has ended up as a pattern. It seems insulting to its fundamental nature to be manipulated with Photoshop. But we must admit that the contrast between the orgiastic/organic/anarchy and the systematic/symmetrical/geometric paradoxically matches together, creating something which, from very far away, could almost look like a classical wallpaper design. Close up, it looks like nothing else ever seen before. The stacking of two layers generates a highly saturated field of lines, looking like a surprising architecture woven by some maniac spider – a highly hypnotic wallpaper!'

Florence Manlik

Florence Manlik was born in 1967 in the north-east of France, and has been living in Paris since 1995. In 2000 she decided to move from pure art to illustration. She still balances her work between the two fields, but her supple and untemporal hand-drawn work has since found its way to a broad range of products, which include book, LP and CD covers, snowboards for K2, clothing, packaging, shop windows for Cacharel and, most recently, wallpaper for Maxalot in Barcelona.

What would you say are the main influences on your work or style? Where do you draw inspiration?
Let's say it's some metaphysical quest with only the help of 0.20 pens. I could spend my life tracing lines on smooth paper. I love the idea of working with almost nothing. Of course there is a computer and his friends, but they usually only do the cleaning, sending and communication work. For this wallpaper they became more playful.

Are there certain things you consider when designing a paper?
I've only made this one, and for an art wallpaper collection, which allows experimental work. The idea was to propose an over-dimensioned pattern, disconcerting but still elegant, airy and hypnotic. I guess it is necessary to watch a certain 'comfort' level, but it is almost impossible to have an idea of someone else's perception, or degree of visual evolution.

To repeat, or not repeat?
I like the quiet, easy, reassuring, calm side of pattern. I like the single artwork for its unique character. I cannot choose, in the absolute, it depends upon the space.

What's the future of wallpaper? How do you see it evolving?
Technically, the future is already here, wallpaper is removable, reusable, magnetic and photographic, and customers can even design it themselves! Now wallpaper should be more democratic, less expensive, as it was during the 1970s, to get the chance of becoming as popular as it was then.

Favourite music to design/work with?
I used to listen to music while drawing, mostly electronic, but now that I have a bird, Cagesan, I prefer to listen to his songs. He doesn't like music except Anne Laplantine; he usually prefers 'natural' sounds like the garbage truck, bus, Hoover ... His debut album 'I love machine' will be released in May 2006 (www.beaubrun.net). His amusing singing is remixed by about 15 electronic artists (of course I'm designing the cover artwork). Cagesan will be the first bird superstar ever, I'm very proud of him!

manlik.florence@neuf.fr
www.manlik.blogspot.com
www.maxalot.com

Virgil Marti

Virgil Marti was born in St Louis, Missouri, USA and lives and works in Philadelphia. He received his BFA from the Washington University School of Fine Arts in 1984, and an MFA from Tyler School of Art, Temple University in 1990. He also attended the Skowhegan School of Painting and Sculpture. One person exhibitions of his work have been held at the Elizabeth Dee Gallery, Holly Solomon Gallery, Thread Waxing Space and Participant (all New York), the Institute of Contemporary Art in Philadelphia and the Santa Monica Museum of Art. Virgil's work is in the collections of the Cooper Hewitt National Design Museum, the New Museum of Contemporary Art, the Whitney Museum of American Art (all New York), the Philadelphia Museum of Art, and the Victoria and Albert Museum, London.

'Bully wallpaper was originally created in 1992 for an installation in the basement boiler room of the Community Education Center – part of the exhibition "Gender Engendered", curated by Jeanne Nugent. Though it reflects the artist's preoccupation with temporal shifts in taste, the subject of the work, writes Jeanne Nugent, is the "adolescent torment of sissies by tough guys". To a French toile wallpaper design, Virgil has added silk-screened photographs of class "bullies" from The Padlock, his junior high school yearbook. Printed in fluorescent inks, the traditional pattern is assaulted by modish treatments whose obsolescence is perhaps best personified by the mid-1970s haircuts. The visual aggression of the pattern is mirrored in the symbolic retribution of the mug-shot portraiture.'

–Richard Torchia

Above left: *Bully* wallpaper installed in the men's room of the Fabric Workshop and Museum, Philadelphia (2003)
Photography: Aaron Igler

Above right: *Bully* installation view at the Wexner Center, Columbus, Ohio in the exhibition 'Apocalyptic Wallpaper' (1997)

Opposite: *Bully* wallpaper (originally printed 1992), screen-print, fluorescent ink and rayon flock on tyvek, blacklights.
Courtesy of the Artist, the Fabric Workshop and Museum and Elizabeth Dee Gallery
Photography: Aaron Igler

...ound out. It is only the superficial qualities that last. Man's deeper nature is soon found out. Wickedness is a myth invented by good people to account for the curious ...ss of others. ...ing that actually occurs is of the smallest importance. Religions...

Opposite: *For Oscar Wilde* installation at Eastern State Penitentiary, Philadelphia. (1995). Part of the exhibition 'Prison Sentences: The Prison as Site, The Prison as Subject' curated by Julie Courtney and Todd Gilens.

Hand-printed wallpapers (pigment on paper-backed cotton sateen)

Photography: Will Brown Courtesy of the Artist, the Fabric Workshop and Museum and Elizabeth Dee Gallery

Above: *Lotus Room* as installed at the Fabric Workshop and Museum, Philadelphia, in the exhibition 'On the Wall' (2003) screen-print. Ink on silver Mylar with digitally printed decals that can be placed on top of the wallpaper.

Photography: Aaron Igler Courtesy of the Artist, the Fabric Workshop and Museum, the Rhode Island School of Design Museum of Art and Elizabeth Dee Gallery

'*For Oscar Wilde* (1995) was made to commemorate the centennial of Wilde's trial and imprisonment. The installation was designed as series of tableaux with increasing degrees of abstraction, in accord with Wilde's ideas about the superiority of the artificial over the natural. Wilde spoke of the sunflower and lily as being the natural forms best suited to design; so the viewer moved from a patch of live sunflowers growing outside, to a field of silk lilies in the cellblock, to a cell wallpapered with those motifs. Ironically, the design of Eastern State Penitentiary somewhat resembles a flower.

Wilde wrote, in letters from prison, that he found the white walls to be one of the most dehumanizing aspects. In an attempt to redress this complaint, I refurbished a cell for him and wallpapered it. Wilde's association with wallpaper is best-known through his alleged deathbed quote: "My wallpaper and I are fighting a duel to the death. One or the other of us has to go."

Lotus Room (2003): Originally created for the exhibition 'On the Wall' at the Rhode Island School of Design Museum of Art, it was inspired by the museum's collection of Japanese Noh robes. The decals allude to early wallpapers, where cut paper branches and sprigs could be applied to disguise cracks and flaws in the wall.'

'*Pills* wallpaper (originally 1994) is flocked wallpaper printed with oversized day-glo images of sleeping pills. Perceptually, the fluorescent colours and blacklights combine to create a space, which seems flattened and cartoon-like but with a contradictory sensation of depth (some colours floating above the surface, some receding). Reminiscent of stained glass. '

What would you say are the main influences on your work or style? Where do you draw inspiration?
I get a lot of inspiration from films. *Last Year at Marienbad* is a big one for me. I also collect and love interior design books and magazines from the 1960s and 1970s.

What do you aim to create with your work?
I try to imbue decoration with an emotional content. I would also like people to get over guilt about visual pleasure.

What inspired you to work with wallpaper? What is it you like about this medium?
Initially, it was a way for me to talk about painting in relation to architecture. It also stemmed from thinking about Warhol's Cows. I like the simplicity and economy of the gesture: you make a material (wallpaper), and then you paste it up until you run out of walls. It's kind of paradoxical: the pattern can be really loud or busy, but it's also very minimal in terms of the gesture.

Are there certain things you consider when designing a paper?
I try to think site-specifically about the place where the paper will be installed. What is the architecture like, what is the history of the place, what is the function of the place?

What do you dislike with a passion?
Pretentiousness.

For you, is wallpaper art or décor, or both?
I would say it could be either, depending on the context. I'm interested in trying to present it as art, but I also like that it can sort of collapse (like a soufflé) and be just wallpaper.

Left: *Pills* (1999): Fluorescent flocked wallpaper, blacklights Installation at the Jerwood Gallery, London in the exhibition 'Natural Dependency' curated by Stephen Hepworth (1999)

www.elizabethdeegallery.com

Geoff McFetridge

Graphic designer, animator, filmmaker, and 'all-around visual auteur', Geoff McFetridge was born in Calgary, Canada, and lives and works in Los Angeles. He began his career as Art Director of the seminal Beastie Boys' magazine *Grand Royal* and went on to establish his own company, Champion Graphics, in 1996. His work covers a wide area including illustrations and logos for Milk Fed, design work for Stüssy and Burton, package design for Gasbook 9 and textiles for Marc Jacobs. He has fashioned products for Nike, and will be launching his own skateboard company, dubbed Atwater. Geoff is also a founding member of The Directors Bureau alongside Mike Mills, Sofia Coppola and Shynola and created the opening title sequences for such Hollywood movies as *Adaptation* and *The Virgin Suicides* as well as music videos for the Avalanches, Simian and Plaid.

What turns you on as an artist? What do you really like?
I really like having my mind blown. Out the back, out through my ears or dripping out my eye sockets etc.

What inspired you to work with wallpaper?
Originally, the thought was to do a continuous poster. I was doing shows where I would cover the gallery walls with posters, end to end, the entire gallery. The wallpaper was an extension of this. I had it on large dispensers and people could rip off bits that they wanted.

What do you always notice or look for when you enter a space?
Like 'the first thing people see is your shoes' type of thing? I'm not sure. I like to look at what books people have. That is always interesting. It can say a lot about someone – unless they own a bookshop.

Less is more? Or blast the place with colour and pattern?
My wallpaper is insane. I don't know if I could live with it every day. I like a lot of primary colour though. I like eclectic. Someone has to bring back the saying 'co-ordination kills'.

Opposite: *Shadows of the Paranormal*
Above: *Stoner Forest*
Left: *Insect*

Above: *Dead Trees*
Opposite: *Nike Vandal Stripe*

For you, is wallpaper art or décor, or both?
I think it is both. Definitely, after I first made wallpaper, I was shocked how 'décor' it was. Even though my paper is hand-printed and some of the film is even cut by hand, it was interesting to see how it was not valued the same as a poster printed the same way. Same as T-shirt screens are not valued the same as a silkscreen on paper. The amount of effort put into something and its value are often at odds. The danger of that is when handmade things disappear, nobody cares. I watch this happening with skateboards, surfboards and bicycles. I think computer-printed wallpaper is gross.

What's the future of wallpaper?
I think that wallpaper is quite grounded in tradition. Wallpaper looks best in rooms with a lot of detail – like a château or an apartment in Paris. Which is ironic since the people interested in it now are sort of design-oriented people, many of whom live in modern homes. In Los Angeles the millions, of tract homes may get into wallpaper soon, but it will be Tuscan, faux-finished, beige weirdness. When the trendsetters start to buy tract homes, that will be interesting.

Is there something you are most proud of?
My daughter, and I made her a play kitchen that we both love.

Laur Meyrieux

Born in France, Laur Meyrieux works independently as an interior designer and artist. She began working in Paris, and then moved to live and work in Tokyo in June 2002. Laur co-founded the design unit Postnormal and her creations span from interior design, exhibition design, art direction, art installation and graphic design to photography. Her work is recognized for its unique style: simple, strong and feminine. Laur actively collaborates with international creators: musicians, video artists, designers, fashion designers, dancers and so forth. She received the prestigious Frame award (*Frame magazine*) for best installation during Tokyo Designers Block 2004.

Restir Boutique Tokyo Ginza, Japan (2005): 'The concept for this project was to create a chic, unique and comfortable environment. For the wallpaper, I mixed classical reference with "trash texture". With the large print image, I combined the classical reference of the painting *Aurora* (a fresco in Rome from 1613) with a "trash" texture (like a bad copy machine). The texture offers two different visions – when we are close we see the "trash treatment" – dots of the image that really appear like a texture. And when we are at the opposite end of the shop we see the total image as a fresco on a wall. This painting is really strong; there is a real perspective, a dynamic we can have in architecture. *Aurore* meaning "day break" has also a symbolic force, puissance, full of hope ...'

Restir Boutique Kobe, Japan (2005): 'Luxury fashion boutique, *Restir Kobe* is based on the same concept as *Restir Tokyo Ginza*. The large image is composed of flower and pattern both with different textures; like Ginza, it offers two different visions (from far and close). The wallpaper with pattern is printed with dark grey colour on black, which offers a subtle nuance. The wallpaper on projection brings light for the cashier – the graphic appears on the wall as well as on the face of the staff at the cash desk. For me it was a different medium on which to show wallpaper.'

Opposite, above:
Restir Boutique Kobe (2005)
Wallpaper image (flower and pattern) with graphic texture (size 6.6 m x 1.8 m)
Photography: Kozo Takayama

Opposite, below:
Wallpaper projection

Top: *Restir Boutique Tokyo Ginza* (2005)
Wallpaper image with graphic texture (size 4.7 m x 2.3 m)

Above: *Restir Boutique Tokyo Ginza* (2005)
Photography: Mote Sinabel

What would you say are the main influences on your work or style? Where do you draw inspiration?
Life, travel, curiosity. I keep my eyes open to see what's happening and keep a notebook and small camera with me in my bag all the time.

Artists/designers/people you admire most?
I'm really interested in artists more than designers. Artists working with space like Dan Graham, Bruce Nauman, Donald Judd, Dan Flavin, Jenny Holzer, Vanessa Beecroft and more. As a graphic designer I am quite impressed with M/M Paris.

Are there certain things you consider when designing a paper?
Space, colour, texture.

What's your preferred method of production and materials?
Computer. Most of the time the bases are photos I've taken.

What do you always notice or look for when you enter a space?
Lighting, colour, atmosphere.

To repeat, or not repeat?
Never repeat.

Favourite music to design/work with?
Most of the time something dynamic … rock/punk music.

Opposite and above: *Blanco Hair Salon Tokyo Aoyama,* Japan (2000)
Pattern on movable panel
Photo image in monochrome with video line texture

Blanco Hair Salon – Tokyo Aoyama, Japan (2000): 'The wallpaper image is like an extension of the garden which appears from the large window. To give a vision between reality and fiction, the image shows two people (human scale) walking in a garden. The texture for the wallpaper is similar to the texture of a video image. The wallpaper on the panel is decorative. The panel can move easily to have a different display inside the space and we can also change the wallpaper to give a different atmosphere.'

laur.lola@gmail.com

Above: *Chambre avec vue*

'*Chambre avec vue*, produced by Maxalot, is designed to disorient the flatness of wall and space. My goal was to create something that almost camouflages the spatial structure. The theme is also about the mathematical deconstruction of space. I was imagining and playing with the idea of an engine that functions with the energy of prime numbers – their godliness qualities and significance. I also wanted to challenge the medium of wallpaper. I did not want the design to be something in the background, to nicely blend in and be ignored. I wanted something almost oppressing, unnerving or overpowering. Wallpaper is powerful enough that, as you look at it, it looks back at you. I wanted the sense that it is something majestic, which is viewing and observing you – viewing the room as in a way that room is viewing you.'

Kenzo Minami

Originally from Kobe, Japan, Kenzo graduated from Parsons School of Design, New York with a BFA in product design after studying western philosophy in Japan. He started his career as a set designer for TV, which led him to shoot his own shorts and TV spots. Eventually he started his activities as an artist and was featured in multiple publications and shows (including his first solo show 'Codex 408' in SoHo, New York), and his work has been commissioned by many clients around the world. He is featured in the Reebok ad campaign 'I am what I am' among Jay-Z, 50 cent, Lucy Liu, Christina Ricci and others. As one of the selected few artists for its 'Artist Series', he released his own model of Reebok Pump Fury, limited to 500 pairs worldwide, in autumn 2005. He also started his own garment project line in spring 2004.

Was there a defining moment when you decided to become a designer?
As long as I can remember, I was drawing or making something and at some point in my life, people started calling me a designer and started sending me cheques for it. So I guess it is easier for me to remember the defining moment when 'they' decided that I was a designer…

What inspired you to work with wallpaper? What is it you like about this medium?
I love the fact that it is something that takes so much commitment as a design element in our daily lives – much more than our clothes, shoes or cars. It becomes so much a statement of ourselves as well as our taste, and we literally have to live with it. It takes a certain level of fine balance to choose one – you want your taste reflected, but not to the extent that you have to stare at the very core of your own psyche 24 hours a day.

What do you always notice or look for when you enter a space?
How particular elements in the space catch your eye to become almost a starting point or trigger, and guide your eyes in a particular direction. This creates a certain flow and essentially manipulates our way of interacting with the space we are entering.

What do you dislike with a passion?
Mediocrity.

Is there something you are most proud of?
That I survived living in New York City half of my life and still do not have a number for a shrink on my speed dial or any addictions whatsoever.

www.kenzominami.com
www.cwc-i.com
www.maxalot.com

Nice

Based in London, design and illustration service Nice (Sofie Eliasson and Matt Duckett) find inspiration in everything from 'greasy spoon' interiors to Kinder Eggs and ceramic animals found in car boot sales. With ideas taken from everyday life and some taken out of thin air, Nice aim to inject humour into their image making. Always aiming to try something new, they particularly like exploring different ways of applying their designs – whether it is on bespoke interiors like wallpaper or tiles, fashion prints or record covers.

'The *Hybrid* wallpaper range is a self-initiated project that consists of four designs: *Mammals, Insects, Sea Creatures* and *Reptiles.* The collection looks to push the concept of wallpaper by making the consumer part of the design process as it allows for a number of unique patterns to be created using one or a combination of the four designs.'

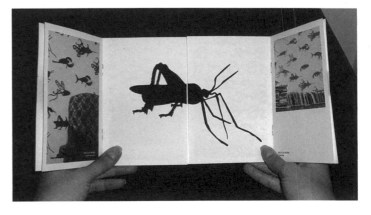

Left: *Sea Creatures, Mammals* and *Insects*

Right: *Hybrid* wallpaper collection catalogue

'The *Peacock* repeat design was produced as a reaction to the more graphic wallpapers Nice have designed before. The idea was to produce something that was decorative but simple.'

Where do you live and create your work?
We have a studio, but we get our best ideas when we're out and about.

What turns you on as artists? What do you really like?
Everything from fashion and interiors to Arnold Schwarzenegger films.

What do you aim to create with your work?
We like to make people think about their environment. So the viewer can become the creator themselves.

What inspired you to work with wallpaper? What is it you like about this medium?
We both like the fact that it is an old and traditional medium but felt it was a great platform for designing something contemporary.

Do you have an ideal dream project? What would you most like to do?
Every job brings up its own challenges, but decorating the London Underground would be nice. (You did say 'dream')

What do you always notice or look for when you enter a space?
Where's the TV? (Sorry, it's true)

What do you most dislike?
Linda Barker, computers, tubes, estate agents; the list could go on and on.

How would you like your own work to develop?
We'd like to move into different areas of interior design. Tiling is something we're working on at the moment.

Opposite and above: *Peacock*

sales@niceness.co.uk
www.niceness.co.uk

Omnivore Inc.

Karen Hsu received a BFA in graphic design from Oregon State University and an MFA in graphic design from Yale University School of Art. She co-founded Omnivore, Inc. with Alice Chung in 2002. Karen was one of *Print* magazine's 2003 New Visual Artists and had two projects designed while working at 2x4, Inc. featured in the 2003 Cooper Hewitt National Design Museum Triennial exhibition. She is a visiting critic with the Yale University School of Art graduate graphic design program.

What would you say are the main influences on your work or style? Where do you draw inspiration?
I am probably most influenced by my environment. I began creating wallpaper concepts while living in my first New York City studio apartment, which was so tiny and dark. Personal experiences and stories combined with the desire to embellish a confined space provide the best inspiration.

Artists/designers/people you admire most?
'Buffy the Vampire Slayer' was my favourite figure through my 20s. I love horror films. I love my pets. I love and have incredible respect for my husband's creative vision and logic.

Was there a defining moment when you decided to become a designer?
At Oregon State University my freshman year, I chickened out of signing up for fine art and then illustration was no longer offered as a major due to budget cuts. I fell into design by accident, but when I look back, it was so appropriate. In high school I made posters for the drama department, helped with the newspaper and literary magazine layouts. In a sense, graphic design was something I was doing before I ever realized it was a professional pursuit.

What do you aim to create with your work?
Is it terrible if I just want to make something that I like?

What inspired you to work with wallpaper? What is it you like about this medium?
Home is important to me. I like how wallpaper is decorative but it can transform a space. I like how it is inherently/traditionally feminine, as part of the interior of a home.

Preferred method of production and materials?
I like to draw directly in Illustrator, with my mouse.

What's the future of wallpaper? How do you see it evolving?
I imagine it would be great if one could change one's walls as easily as one chooses a different computer wallpaper.

Favourite music to design/work with?
Television!

Opposite: *Tiki Fruit*
Left: *Yellow Fever*

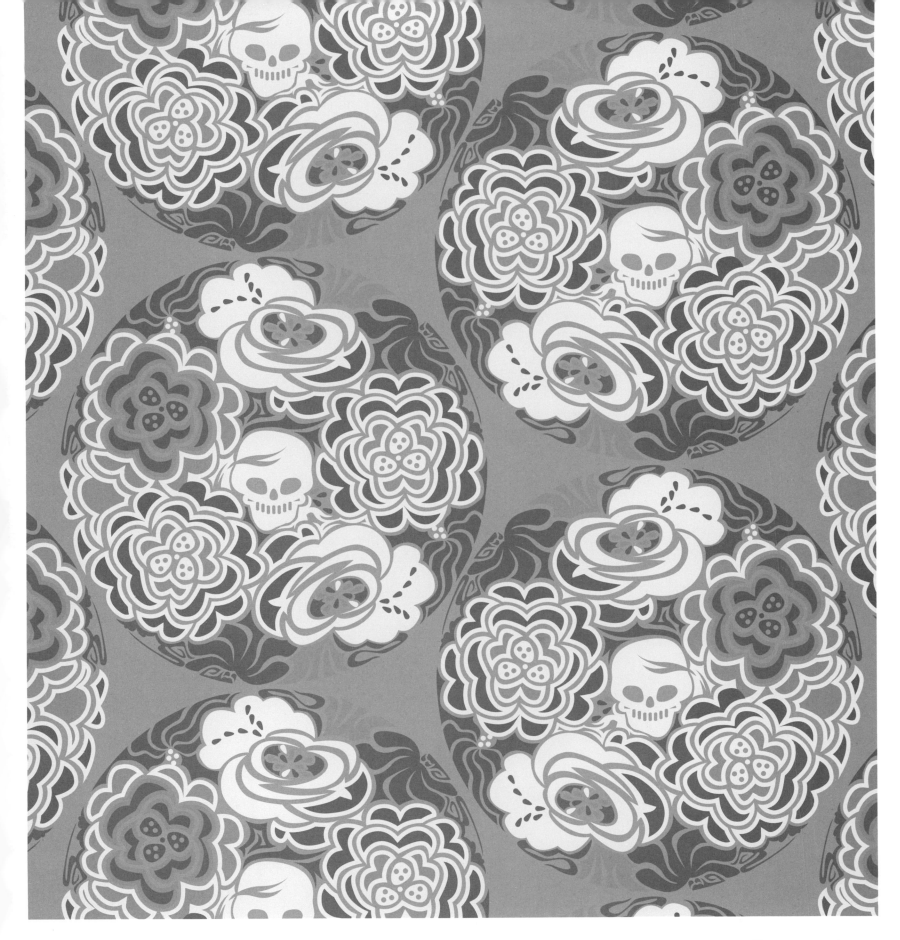

Opposite: *Chula, Charles, and Friends*
Above: *Skull Flower*

All patterns are personal,
non-client-based illustrations by
Karen Hsu

karen@omnivorous.org
www.omnivorous.org

Christopher Pearson

Born in Hong Kong in 1977, Christopher Pearson studied graphic design at Camberwell College of Arts, London and later received an MA in communications art & design at the Royal College of Art, London. In 2001, he joined the Alexander McQueen studio, for which he designed printed textiles and graphics. Under the direction of Interfield Design, he has worked on motion-based projects for BBC1, BBC2, Channel 4, Puma and Bloomberg. Personal clients have included AMEX, Armani, Channel 5, Cartoon Network, Emap, ICA, Graham & Brown, Lucky Strike and Rafael Lopez.

'*Environment Sensitive Wallpaper* is a reworked version of the 1887 William Morris design, *Willow Boughs,* to create a physical wallpaper that will change pattern depending on room temperature and UV exposure.'

Digital Wallpaper installed on wall-sized screens or using projectors is a delicately animating pattern and narrative within the original design. The frequency between animated events varies, from long, motionless pauses, to obscure and unpredictable events, creating a dialogue between viewer and wallpaper. It illustrates the huge diversity of possibility that animated wallpaper offers, ranging from gratuitous eye candy to a sophisticated technology for communication.

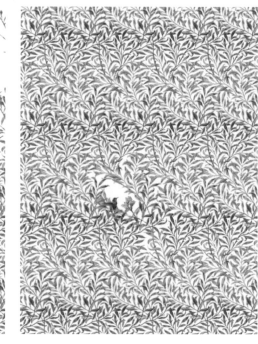

Opposite: *Environment Sensitive Wallpaper*

Above: *Digital Wallpaper* installation, Royal College of Art, London (2005)

Left: *Digital Wallpaper* stills, 'Willow Boughs' designed by William Morris, 1887 *Wallpaper*

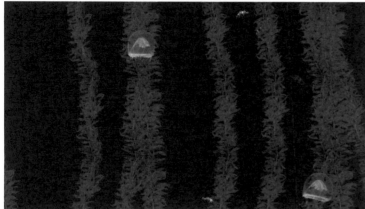
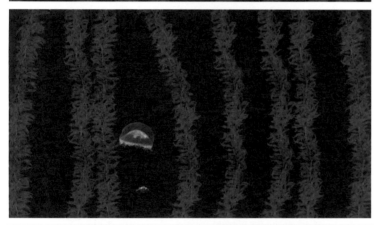
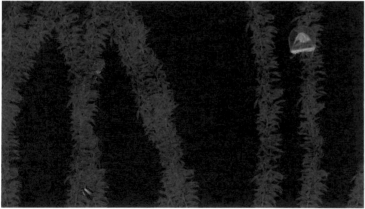

Opposite: Sketch Gallery, London
Above: *Morris* (2005)

Artists/designers/people you admire most?
William Morris – I have animated his *Willow Boughs* wallpaper of 1887. I have found myself going back to his ideas many times to look at how my own work can try to fit with our current version of the 'industrial revolution' – the digital revolution. Also, Heath Robinson, Hayao Miyazaki, Takeshi Kitano, Tom Friedman, Eley Kishimoto and Alexander McQueen.

What do you aim to create with your work?
My recent work plays on the perception of traditional aesthetic and human characteristics to create an alternative approach to the use of digital technology. I am also very interested in the multi-functionality of objects, wallpaper that not only functions as wallpaper but also communicates, teaches, entertains – the possibilities are endless ...

What inspired you to work with wallpaper? What is it you like about this medium?
I worked in textile design for Alexander McQueen for three years; I got a taste for patterning. Wallpaper became my own outlet for working with pattern, it also embodied my interests in traditional design and gave me a structure in which I could explore and find out what wallpaper could be, rather than what people make it.

Do you have an ideal dream project? What would you most like to do?
I am quietly watching the development of e-paper and polymer screens. I hope to cover the inside and outside of a traditional old church, creating a fully interactive surface that plays on the architecture, patterning, stonework, furniture, so that the old and new merge creating an infinite series of detailed experiences.

To repeat, or not repeat?
I love the structure of a repeat; it creates a challenge of making something controlled seem free.

The whole room, or feature walls?
Why stop at a room, why not a building, cars ...? That's the problem with wallpaper, people think it's just for walls; it should be an excuse to cover anything and everything.

What's the future of wallpaper? How do you see it evolving?
Walls are a natural extension for the display screen and surface and natural progression for interface. Walls will become animated, along with many other surfaces.

info@christopherpearson.com
www.christopherpearson.com

Persijn Broersen and Margit Lukács

Persijn Broersen and Margit Lukács are an artist-duo based in Amsterdam, the Netherlands. They met at the Rietveld Academy, Amsterdam where they studied graphic design and graduated at the Sandberg Institute, Amsterdam in 2001 with a masters in design and free arts. Their artistic practice ranges from video installations, drawings, murals and films to commercials and video clips. They deliberately choose to operate in the domain of autonomous visual arts as well as in the world of applied projects to reach a varied audience and to investigate different forms of communication.

'During winter 2003 we lived in a small village in Spain (Calossa d'en Sarria). Next to our house there was a big rocky hill, which we used to climb every morning. We made about 2,000 photos of all the vegetation on the hill. The flora we were particularly interested in had the symmetric, almost monstrous look of some of the plants on the mountain, with strange alien-like fruits seeming to grow as fungus. The drawings we made were both drawn from life as well as from these pictures. We decided then to make a structure of these drawings, which would degenerate into chaos. These plants with their uncontrollable behaviour (unstoppable growing processes) seemed to us a metaphor for the jungle of the outside world. This finally resulted in the *Zwart Licht* (Black Light) wallpaper.

The first time we showed this pattern was during an exhibition in 'de Nieuwe Vide' in Haarlem, the Netherlands, where we completely wallpapered one room. We designed the wallpaper in a time-related manner: the wallpaper develops from one corner to the other. At first sight when you enter the room, it looks like a regular, even classical pattern, but then, starting in the corners and spreading over the other walls the pattern gets mouldy, the flowers and plant-like structures grow wild and disturb the pattern and black holes start to appear. An example of entropy.'

Opposite: *Zwart Licht* detail
Right: *Zwart Licht*

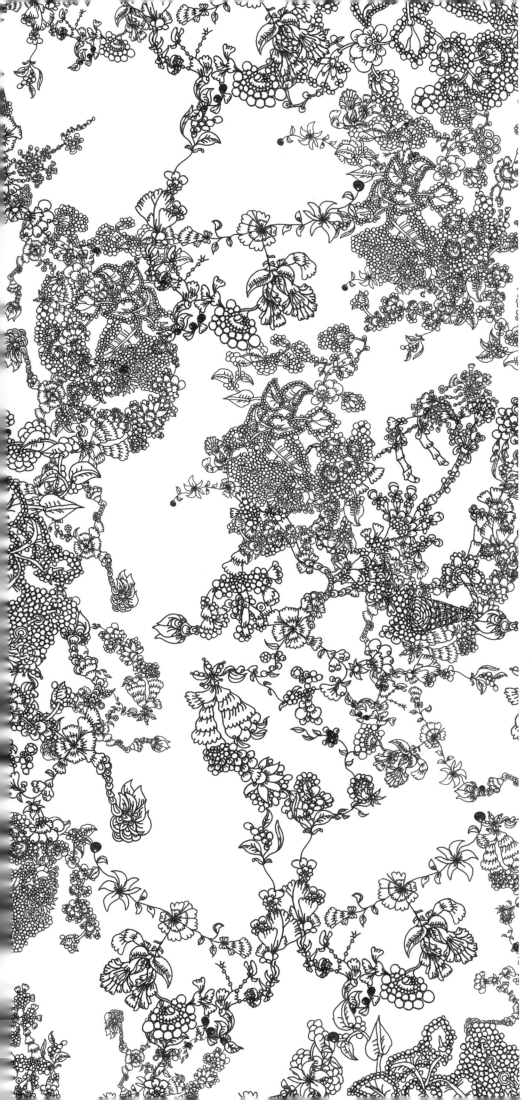

What turns you on as artists? What do you really like?
The beauty and obscenity of nature.

What inspired you to work with wallpaper? What is it you like about this medium?
We see a similarity between wallpaper and the way we experience media. It's both something you take for granted but it doesn't stick to your mind. It's there, but it's also invisible. In a way you can get lost in a pattern; like reading the newspaper daily – the news is repeating itself and there's no way out, but you go over it day in and day out as a routine, and you react in a routine. You forget there is a pattern. Also the lack of frame is something we like. Wallpaper/pattern is surrounding you from all sides and makes you almost physically feel you're in a jungle.

Are there certain things you consider when designing a paper?
Yes, scale, time development, movement, shift of perspective, the friction between chaos and order, the (non)visibility or clarity of a possible pattern.

Do you have an ideal dream project? What would you most like to do?
Make a sad and very touching musical from the book *Les yeux sont faits* by Jean-Paul Sartre. Also we really would like one day to design patterns for Victor & Rolf.

What do you always notice or look for when you enter a space?
Accidental coincidence in carelessly decorated interiors, we like the beauty of that.

Opposite: *Zwart Licht Kentucky*
Left: *Flower Wall*

pm@pmpmpm.com
www.pmpmpm.com

Above: *From Hell with Love* (2005) Exposif wallpapers, Maxalot

info@phunkstudio.com
www.phunkstudio.com
www.maxalot.com

Phunk Studio

Alvin Tan, Melvin Chee, Jackson Tan and William Chan met in Lasalle-SIA College of the Arts and came together in 1994 to form Phunk Studio, a creative collective in Singapore described by Creative Review as 'the champion of Singapore's graphic scene'. Their cross-disciplinary approach is best described as 'an aesthetic collective consciousness' focused on experimenting with new approaches to visual expressions. Phunk has collaborated and worked with international brands such as Nike, MTV, Daimler Chrysler, Diesel, Levis, Comme des Garçons, Tiger Beer and Salem. Their self-published multi-media project entitled *Transmission* was distributed worldwide, showcasing the works of Phunk and their collaborators from around the world. They have exhibited and lectured in New York, London, Sydney, Berlin, Valencia, Shanghai, Taipei, Ecuador, Gwangju, Kuala Lumpur and Singapore. Phunk has been featured in numerous international books and magazines such as I.D. (International Design), *Tokion*, *XLR8R*, *Studio Voice*, *+81*, *Mass Appeal*, *IDN*, *Black + White* and *Soma*.

From Hell with Love is based on another of Phunk Studio's famous artworks *Control Chaos*. It is a place influenced by the pugilistic world of 1980s Hong Kong TV serials, ancient mythology tales such as *Journey to the West* and *The 18 Chambers of Hell* and childhood visits to Haw Par Villa. Phunk has injected its distinctive style of illustration and urban street culture iconography into these tales. It renders Phunk's own dysfunctional/apocalyptic take on the classic tales of good versus evil set against the backdrop of heaven, earth and hell.

Artists/designers/people you admire most?
Lee Kuan Yew, Michael Jordan, Peter Saville, Wong Kar Wai, Frank Miller, Andy Warhol, Saul Bass ... and many more.

What turns you on as artists? What do you really like?
The collective creative spirit.

Do you have an ideal dream project? What would you most like to do?
Design a pattern as distinctive as the houndstooth, a typeface as widely used as Helvetica and a book as widely read as the Bible.

What do you dislike with a passion?
A dirty floor.

How would you like your own work to develop?
More content, less packaging.

Is there something you are most proud of?
A decade of decadence.

Jo Pierce

Jo Pierce completed an MA in design for textile futures at Central Saint Martins College of Art & Design, London in 2003. She created *Re-surface* design with a desire to produce surface design that would merge crafted sensibilities with high tech processes – contrasting both the old and the new in materials, techniques and production and using processes to include screen-printing, digital printing, stitch and graffiti stencil.

Re-surface design is concerned with creating contemporary crafted design for the interior, producing individual, bespoke experiences in wallpaper and fabric. Handmade pieces are created that locate between craft and technology, art and design.

Jo creates designs from collected images, drawings and objects collaged together, re-contextualizing found fragments into new compositions to create stories and landscapes on the wall and on fabric.

Re:wallpaper is a collection of handmade, bespoke wallpapers. The wallpapers include directions for the consumer, with instructions such as 'cut out', 'fill' or 'peel' – encouraging the owner to partake, change and transform their wallpaper and thus create a more personal connection with the product. The participant is encouraged to collage and add their own images and can paint in their own colour (cut'n'fill) in order to have a distinctly individual interior.

Opposite: *Cut'n'fill*
Top: *Embroidery*
Left: *Embroidery* detail

'*Aeroplane* is a further use of reinvention. This paper is developed from the idea of reworking old and existing wallpapers with new pattern. Screen-printed onto the top of the original paper, the falling paper planes tumble to the ground. This is also the same for the laser planes (pattern cut by laser) apart from the pattern, which is cut out to expose the paper layered underneath. It developed from the enjoyment of peeling wallpaper to discover what lies underneath! '

What would you say are the main influences on your work or style? Where do you draw inspiration?
I love the qualities of collage, putting seemingly random things together to create a dialogue. I love cutting things out and pasting them together. Almost like a scrap book, but also combined with drawing, stitch and print.

Artists/designers/people you admire most?
Dutch designer, Hella Jongerious. She is always working on different surface/scale/materials and always breaking conventions in a playful way.

What turns you on as an artist? What do you really like?
Unwanted things, ornaments, old recipe books and gardening books, etc. I love to bring new life to something, not just by using it but maybe photographing it, painting it or putting it into a new context.

What do you aim to create with your work?
Most of my work is still quite experimental, playful with the medium of wallpaper. I want to find new ways of using wallpaper, adapting it to uses other than decoration – maybe as a creative tool, or a way to tell personal stories in an interior space, to make the space unique and individual.

What inspired you to work with wallpaper? What is it you like about this medium?
Size, scale, flatness and the way it becomes embedded into the interior. Wallpaper is less formal than a painting; it moves round corners, goes in the back of cupboards and everybody has some memory of it. It's more approachable. When I first saw the wallpapers at Salterton House in Devon I was totally inspired to add bits, cut bits in and lay pieces over the top to create individual landscapes.

What do you most dislike?
Too much perfection.

Opposite: Laser cut *Aeroplane*
Above: *Aeroplane*

jo@re-surfacedesign.com
www.re-surfacedesign.com

Above: *Landscape one*

PixelNouveau
(Diego Vargas Sales)

Diego Vargas Sales was born in Costa Rica in 1980 and studied architecture and urbanism in San Jose, Costa Rica as well as drawing lessons and alternative materials with Costa Rican artist Joaquin Rodrigues del Paso. After leaving the architecture major he became a self-taught graphic computer artist. His first work as a designer was for Mäe 'fashion, art and entertainment'. He produced advertising and promotional products with Costa Rican designers Marco Kelso and Rocket, while continuing his self-taught education in vectorial illustration and other forms of painting and drawing. He also became involved with the collective group of painters called 'Taller Rosa' (Pink Workshop). By using applications of 'video triggering' and post-production as an experiment, he also made video material for electronic music at both Costa Rican and international events with visual performances of live video VJing. He has worked in advertising agency Jotabeq Grey and as a freelance graphic designer.

'These two pieces *Landscape one* and *two* were created as part of the collection of wallpapers offered by Maxalot. This project consists of two graphic pieces of impossible and absurd landscapes. They both are part of a collection of images or rather a group ensemble of irreverent elements and characters. Everything revolves around interpretation. Constantly interpreting codes and symbols, it's via the ambiguity of the symbols and in the creation of a unique piece for every spectator that the work is interpreted by its self-references.'

What would you say are the main influences on your work or style? Where do you draw inspiration?
One of my main influences has been Ignacio Quiros, a Costa Rican painter and personal friend of mine. I was also inspired by the character of Dean Moriarty from the book *On the Road*, by Jack Kerouac. And 1980s video clips.

Artists/designers/people you admire most?
I admire Richard D. James, Geoff Lillemon and Matthew Barney as creators.

Was there a defining moment when you decided to become a designer?
When I was a child, my mother had an old reproduction of *Jane Avril*, by Toulouse-Lautrec; I use to stare at it for hours. I think it was then that I knew I wanted to be an artist.

What's your preferred method of production and materials?
My work is a result of a combined use of photography, painting and montage, all done digitally.

Do you have an ideal dream project? What would you most like to do?
I would like to do a theatre piece and create a fusion with music, video projections and multi-media.

Less is more? Or blast the place with colour and pattern?
In my work, I always try to saturate with meaning. Although my work is filled with colour and variation of elements, nothing is there by mistake; there is no element within its composition that is not justified. This is the most important thing to have in consideration when doing any piece, knowing that everything within it has meaning.

Favourite music to design/work with?
To illustrate scenarios, I listen to the epic or abstract such as John Cage.

Above: *Landscape two*

esteviernes@gmail.com
www.pixelnouveau.com
www.maxalot.com

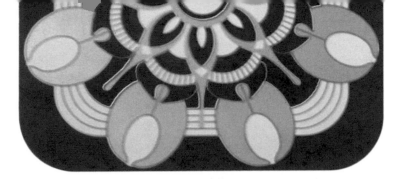

Publisher Textiles

Mark and Rhynie Cawood established Publisher Textiles, a Sydney-based textile and wallpaper company in 2002. All their designs are hand-printed in-house. Mark's background in screen-printing and teaching textile design, and Rhynie's background in fashion, meant they primarily designed and printed fabrics for a range of fashion and interior products. In 2003 they were commissioned to custom design and produce outrageously flamboyant wallpaper for The Ruby Rabbit, a bar in Sydney. This was their first venture into making their own wallpaper and from that came more commercial commissioned projects for various bars, restaurants and boutiques. Now Publisher Textiles wallpapers also cater for the homewares market. Their influences include the organic forms of art nouveau, the charm of tribal artwork, and the foresight of science fiction, to name a few.

'Roto was commissioned by an interior designer (Caroline Choker of DS17), for a Café in Newtown, Sydney called Hoochie Mamma. Inspired by retro styles, African forms and vintage aeroplane motors, this bold geometric print covers one wall and a ceiling recess. The rest of the interiors in the café are dark, and this really makes the wallpaper spring to life.'

Opposite and left: *Roto* (2005)
created by Mark Cawood

'*Bugsey* was inspired by the framework in insect wings and futuristic shapes. It can give a room many different personas, depending on the furniture and pieces put with it. It has been used in a day spa accompanied by Indian artefacts, and then again in a living room filled with Danish-style furniture.

Drake was created first for fashion and then transcended to wallpaper. Inspired by Aubrey Beardsley and art nouveau illustrations, together with natural silhouettes, *Drake* can either create a textural backdrop when used in soft colours, or it can be quite dramatic. It has recently been used in black and white to cover the foyer of an art deco style apartment, which has included a previously dead space into the rest of the apartment.'

Where do you live and create your work?
We have a design studio and factory where we create and produce wallpapers and fabrics by hand. Presently there are three artist/designers (Mark, Rhynie and Aidan Thrum) who are also involved in the production.

What do you aim to create?
This is really just an outlet for our imagination. We hope to create an atmosphere or emotion – calming, energizing, etc. We cater for different moods with small subtle prints, which create a decorative texture, or bold graphic lines for a dramatic impact. Colour also plays a very important role. It can change an outrageous and bold print into a textural background.

What's your preferred method of production and materials?
All our wallpapers are hand screen-printed in-house. Surprisingly, this method, although very laborious and time consuming, provides a lot of freedom. It is also the basis to other methods like flocking and foiling, as these use block-printing, which is very similar to screen-printing. We generally use a paper base to keep the price affordable, but quite often for commercial projects, vinyl is used.

What do you dislike with a passion?
Catalogue homes!!!!! There is nothing more unattractive than going into a house that is filled with the same furniture and accessories as the window of a furniture showroom, and is just like the one next door. There seems to be a soulless formula that so many people follow, void of sentimental or precious pieces.

Do you have an ideal dream project? What would you most like to do?
Yes – but it's a secret …

Opposite and left: *Bugsey* (2004) created by Mark Cawood

Top: *Drake* (2005) created by Rhynie Cawood

info@publishertextiles.com.au
www.publishertextiles.com.au

Lyn Randall

Lyn Randall returned to full-time education at the age of 30. Training in both Brighton and Buckinghamshire, she graduated in 2004 with a BA (Hons) in textile and surface design. While still training she exhibited work at Indigo in Paris, Surtex in New York, and went on to design, produce and style six complete costumes for Formica and the 2004 launch of their *Collection* range. Lyn has continued to develop her work and has exhibited at a number of London exhibitions, including New Designers Exhibition 2004 at the Business Design Centre, New Designers Selection at the Gainsborough Studios, Urban Interiors Exhibition and the forthcoming *House & Garden* Fair 2006 as part of the 'Women on a Roll' Installation. Lyn's work is displayed at the contemporary Interior Gallery/Showroom Cho Cho San in Islington, London, through which she receives bespoke orders for interior design pieces.

Identity of Place – White on White Wall Piece (total length approx 300 mm x 3,000 mm) in layered, stitched and embossed vinyl. The piece is based on the ripped and torn wallpapers of derelict rooms and the history of a dwelling.

What would you say are the main influences on your work or style? Where do you draw inspiration?
I am constantly inspired by beauty in the unexpected, e.g. the delicacy of flaking paint on old doorframes, the intrigue of ripped and layered wallpapers in forgotten rooms, the rainbow of subtle colours in the rust on a gate panel – the detail of the commonly overlooked.

Was there a defining moment when you decided to become a designer?
I had always been a creative person, but after working in an office for over ten years I decided I should take the plunge and return to full-time education to study design at the age of 30; I have never looked back.

What turns you on as an artist? What do you really like?
I love delicacy and detail – not fussiness, but a natural pureness that can come from informed and thoughtful design.

What do you aim to create with your work?
Texture and a piece that people want to get closer to touch and interact with.

What inspired you to work with wallpaper? What is it you like about this medium?
I love how it can be interpreted in so many ways; contemporary wall coverings are far removed from the classical flock or woodchip. I love the look and feel of layering identities when rooms are renovated and strips of wallpaper are ripped to reveal glimpses of past times.

What's the future of wallpaper? How do you see it evolving?
Socially, graphically and culturally people have many merging identities and they bring together a myriad of influences to create uniqueness. We want what we put in our homes to reflect this. Wallpaper will be less mass production and more mass individuality.

What do you most dislike?
Extreme minimalism.

Do you have an ideal dream project? What would you most like to do?
I would love my pieces to hang somewhere calm and serene, where light and warmth can play on the surface allowing it to change throughout the day.

lyndiloo@dsl.pipex.com

Right: *White on White Wall Piece* (2005), Cho Cho San, Islington, London

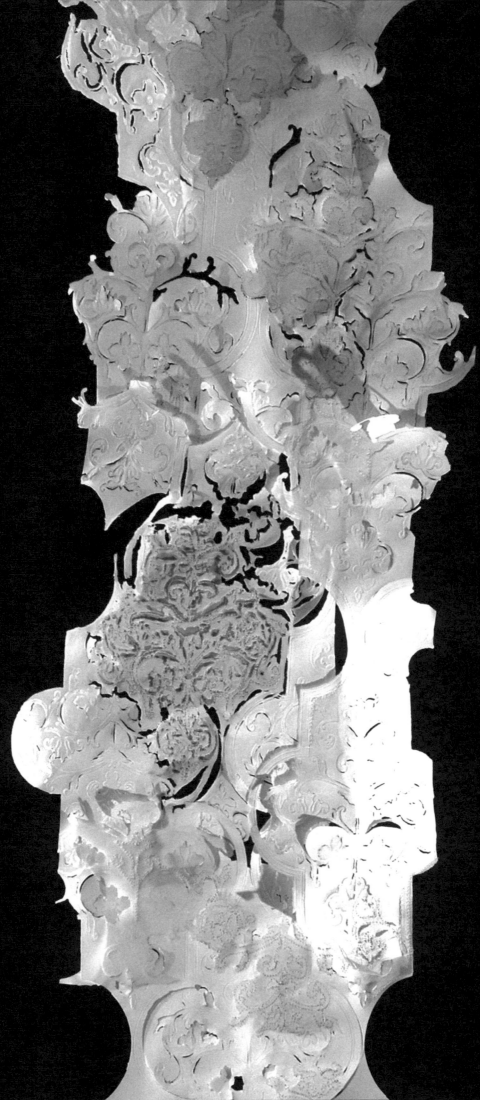

Karim Rashid

Karim Rashid is a leading figure in the fields of product and interior design, fashion, furniture, lighting and art. Born in Cairo, half-Egyptian, half-English, and raised in Canada, Karim now practises in New York. Designing for clients including Umbra, Prada, Miyake and Method, Karim is radically changing the aesthetics of product design and the very nature of the consumer culture. He has had some 2,000 objects put into production and has successfully entered the realm of architecture and interiors with the design of the Morimoto restaurant in Philadelphia and Semiramis hotel in Athens, which won the Sleep05 European Hotel Design Award. His work is in the permanent collections of 14 museums worldwide, including MoMA and SFMoMA, and he exhibits art in various galleries. Karim was an Associate Professor of Industrial Design for ten years and is now a frequent guest lecturer at universities and conferences globally.

The *Replicant* pattern is featured in much of Karim's interior design work, including Askew restaurant in New York, Nooch in Singapore and his personal residence in Chelsea, New York.

Opposite: *Replicant*,
Nooch, Singapore
Photography: CI&A

Above: *Replicant*,
Karim Rashid Loft, New York
Photography:
Jean Francois Jaussaud

Exploring new ways to reference patterning found in nature, Karim digitally generated these designs (*Space Warp, Zenith* and *Flexuous*) for Wolf Gordon and manipulated them to resemble multiple plant, animal, land and human anatomies, as well as forging new ground in 2D pattern making.

Was there a defining moment when you decided to become a designer?
I realized my life's mission at the age of 4. I went sketching with my father in England drawing churches. He taught me to see – he taught me perspective at that age – he taught me that I could design anything and touch all aspects of our physical landscape. I was obsessed with drawing eyeglasses, shoes, radios, luggage, throughout my childhood.

What do you aim to create with your work?
My agenda is to contribute objects in our physical landscape that inspire, engage and encourage positive experiences. I define my work as sensual minimalism, or sensualism, where objects communicate, engage and inspire yet remain fairly minimal. They can speak simply and directly, without superfluousness.

What's your preferred method of production and materials?
I love the digital age as it has afforded us tools that speed up the process, create better precision, better quality, more variance, and the profession is much less hands on, and more in the third order of prosthetics. CNC, Raid prototyping, solid modelling, new production methods, smart materials, parametric programs etc. have really completely shifted the profession.

Do you have an ideal dream project? What would you most like to do?
There is so much to do. I want to design cars, planes, clothes, houses, robots. I want to host a design TV show, I want to create music, I want to design a small museum, I want to live in perpetual inspiration, I want to be smarter, faster, stronger. I want to implant a microchip in my eye that allows me to see everything …

What do you dislike with a passion?
Dishonesty and violence, and the male ego.

What's the future of wallpaper? How do you see it evolving?
I think the future of wallpaper will be 100% biodegradable, eco-friendly, more aesthetic, more colourful and more digital.

Opposite: *Space Warp, Flexuous*
Left: *Zenith*

office@karimrashid.com
www.karimrashid.com

Rinzen

Australian design and art collective Rinzen are best known for their collaborative and illustrative approach, creating utopian alternative realities and other worlds. Rinzen's posters and album covers have been exhibited at the Louvre in Paris and their large-scale artwork installed in Tokyo's Zero Gate and Copenhagen's Hotel Fox. Recent projects include the design of Paul Pope's Batman for DC Comics, graphics for a Bebike bicycle and a Qee for Toy2R. Members of the five-person group are currently based in Sydney, Brisbane and Berlin.

Wallpaper graphics for *Dryads*, Room 307 in the VW Hotel Fox in Copenhagen, Denmark (2005): 'Walking into this room is like wandering into a forest – surrounded by trees, leaves and birds. The intertwining roots of the trees protect small pixie people, the souls of the forest. Throughout the seasons dead leaf matter is drawn down into the earth and sucked up into the roots again. Subtle details are added into the trees that reflect the spirits – like branches that turn into hands, or eyes manifesting in the wood grain. Any which way you turn there is a new story unfolding: a frog playing banjo with his insect band, the fiddle-playing tree, the studious rabbit and his favourite book ...'

Opposite and above: *Dryads*
© Illustration and design: Rinzen
Photography: www.diephotodesigner.de

'*Paradise Project* (2004) was conceived by Kalle Hellzén of Wieden+Kennedy; these three unique wallpaper designs for the agency's Amsterdam offices are intended to contrast the western world's perception of paradise (palm trees, beaches, all-inclusive hotels) with the often starkly non-paradisiacal reality of countries that offer it (poverty, war, genocide, landmines). From afar, the patterns resemble the idyllic artwork of a Hawaiian shirt, but when we move in closer and look into the details, we see the second layer of meaning. The pieces were produced as continuous paper print, and installed as wallpaper at the Amsterdam offices of Wieden+Kennedy in 2004.'

Where do you live and create your work?
Rinzen work from three studios – Brisbane and Sydney and Berlin.

What would you say are the main influences on your work or style? Where do you draw inspiration?
Drawing and dreaming. Other Rinzens. Shockingly new technology, astoundingly old technology.

Artists/designers/people you admire most?
A tiny sampling of our most loved human beings would include Hayao Miyazaki, Jim Henson, Maurice Sendak, Tim Burton, Ricky Swallow, Aubrey Beardsley, Patricia Piccinini, Dali, Picasso, Jean-Michel Basquiat, Hans Bellmer, Chris Ware and Paul Pope.

What inspired you to work with wallpaper? What is it you like about this medium?
It has agreeable connotations of design 'craft', and combines the decorative nature of figurative imagery with the functional aspects of spatial design, to the illumination of both (hopefully).

Preferred method of production and materials?
In terms of final wallpaper production, the thicker the ink the better!

What do you always notice or look for when you enter a space?
My eyes would say the condition of the light, but my memory says the smell.

How would you like your own work to develop?
Hopefully, it will collapse in upon itself and then explode into something new.

Answered by Adrian Clifford, Rinzen

Opposite and left:
Wieden+Kennedy *Paradise Project*
© Concept: Wieden+Kennedy
© Illustration and design: Rinzen

they@rinzen.com
www.rinzen.com

Rob Ryan

Rob Ryan is an illustrator based in Bethnal Green, London who specializes in paper-cut stories. After studying fine art at Trent Polytechnic, Rob continued with printmaking at the Royal College of Art, London and developed his own particular style of hand-cut illustration using paper and scalpel. Rob is happy to transfer his work to whichever medium it suits, which has led to commissions in fields such as book and magazine illustration, album covers and fashion. His clients include Liberty's, Vogue, Penguin, Random House, Bloomsbury, Hodder & Stoughton, Mute Records, Paul Smith, Project Alabama and Sazaby.

'In 2005 I embarked on a collaborative project with Paul Smith, instigated by Alan Aboud of Design Team Aboud Sodano. Paul Smith commissioned a paper-cut illustration to put into a textile print for his *Pink* womenswear range for spring/summer 2006. This range was principally for release in Japan only and comprised a wide range of items, for example hats, umbrellas, bags and purses, jeans, knitwear, cotton jersey, books, ceramics, etc.

The wallpaper that we created was laid out by Lance Martins at Paul Smith and was installed in the Paul Smith Pink Plus shop in the Daikanyama district of Tokyo. I wanted the print to be light and colourful and I suppose I was tailoring my work to be a bit Japanese 'teenage girl-friendly' – but I don't have a problem with that, because I think it looks KAWAII!!! (that's 'cute' in Japanese!)'

What would you say are the main influences on your work or style? Where do you draw inspiration?
I must admit I am a bit of a mess and a fan of everything, I love English illustration: the Erics – Fraser, Ravilious and Gill; Edwards – Bawden and Ardizzone, but I revere Titian and Raphael. Then again I love looking at magazines and fashion – I don't believe that anything is shallow or beneath me being interested in it. Principally though, I draw inspiration from living in a busy place and bustling life itself.

What turns you on as an artist? What do you really like?
A long day in the studio. Having started with one drawing at 8am, redone it with changes by lunchtime, in the mid-afternoon on the third drawing, fresh, new and exciting ideas are coming thick and fast – that's what I really like!

What do you aim to create with your work?
Some form of positive inspiration for the viewer.

What do you always notice or look for when you enter a space?
I suppose it's always people. In say the National Gallery, where you've gone with the expressed intention of looking at the paintings on the wall, I always end up looking at the people looking at the paintings. The paintings are fantastic but the people are the reason the paintings were painted in the first place, so as such are of much more interest.

What do you dislike with a passion?
Pickled things and Nazis.

Is there something you are most proud of?
I'm proud of most of my work but that totally pales into insignificance compared to how proud I am of my daughters Maria and Barbara.

Favourite music to design/work with?
Northern soul, Radio 4, Jonathan Richman, George Jome, Elliott Smith ...

www.misterrob.co.uk

Above and right: Paul Smith's Pink Plus Shop, Daikanyama, Tokyo, Japan

Above: *Gentry Portofino Wallpaper 1*, Italy (2005)

Kustaa Saksi

Illustrator Kustaa Saksi was born in Finland and now lives in Paris, working with various clients in the world of fashion, music and entertainment. His illustrations are a syrupy disarray of elements: playful, paradoxical, often over-glossy, inviting, troubling, messy and yet strangely clear. Saksi combines organic touches and viscous shapes into 'new-world psychedelia'. His work combines his unique imagination with his strict Scandinavian design roots to create a wonderful world of surrealistic landscapes, beautifully strange characters and very strong atmosphere.

Classic Italian cashmere brand Gentry Portofino invited Saksi to make wallpaper designs and patterns to be used on their walls and fabrics, alongside a signature cashmere knitwear collection for spring/summer 2006. The colours of the wallpapers follow the same colour scheme as the knitwear collection. The main theme is sea life: underwater views and imaginative characters; organic and inorganic shapes; simplicity in the chaos; bold shapes and contrasting colours.

Above: Igor Restaurant, Ghent, Belgium (2005)

Parisian fashion department store Printemps commissioned Saksi to design wallpaper for their men's shop on Boulevard Haussmann. The design reflects the contemporary feeling of the first floor department. Because the wallpaper was produced in large scale, Saksi was able to add a lot of elements and details to keep it looking interesting for many years to come.

Where do you draw inspiration?
My friends, cycling, nature, cafés, *magré de canard*, sea, consumer product packaging, summer, Illy coffee, Le Bon Marché, burlesque, Karhu beer, shoe gazing, China Club, scootering, Vodka Martinis, fishing …

Was there a defining moment when you decided to become a designer?
I think I was supposed to be an engineer but then I found psychedelic music.

What turns you on as an artist? What do you really like?
I really like to have a nice dinner.

What do you aim to create with your work?
I try to create as strong an atmosphere as possible.

What inspired you to work with wallpaper? What is it you like about this medium?
It can really take command of a space and it always connects with people.

Do you have an ideal dream project? What would you most like to do?
To direct a burlesque show in Paris.

What do you always notice or look for when you enter a space?
I smell first. That tells a lot about the space.

The whole room, or feature walls?
The whole room – be brave.

For you, is wallpaper art or décor, or both?
100% proud décor. I don't see artistic intentions in wallpaper design.

Favourite music to design / work with?
Classical.

Opposite and left:
Printemps Homme Wallpaper 2,
Boulevard Haussmann fashion store, Paris (2006)

kustaa@kustaasaksi.com
www.kustaasaksi.com

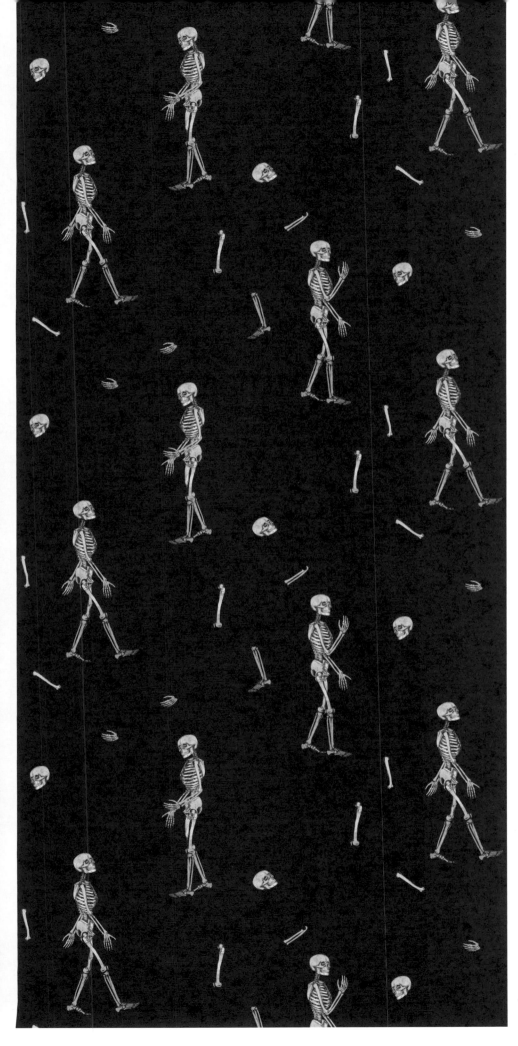

Showroom Dummies

Showroom Dummies are artist Abigail Lane, fashion designer Brigitte Stepputtis and printer Bob Pain. Formed in London in 2003, their exhibition, Interior Motives (Natural Histories and Natural Disasters), was a showcase of their first prototypes, which included wallpaper, tiles and fabrics, printed cashmere blankets, upholstered furniture (by Edwin Wright), macabre concertinaed perspex screens and mirrored dice cube lighting. Showroom Dummies continue to maintain their sometimes unconventional identity with an individual style and approach to commissions and collaboration. Their aim is to make products to a high standard, and to work with a certain flair and aesthetic bravery.

What would you say are the main influences on your work or style?
My interests are long term and therefore the Showroom Dummies style is unlikely to fluctuate with fashions. My love is for circus, natural history, museums, magic and weird shit. My shelves are full of books and magazines on these subjects and I graze and sift from them all the time – armed with post-it notes.

Artists/designers/people you admire most?
I admire anyone brave enough to do his or her own thing and not be pushed around too much by society's desperate need for us all to categorize ourselves. I admire people who, although dedicated to their profession or vision, reach out from their field – and in doing so extend it. I respect Stephen Jay Gould for this, Ricky Jay, Vivienne Westwood and Ian Brown. I like hard-working nerds with a rebellious spirit.

Opposite: Abigail and Ethel with
Skeleton wallpaper, Hackney Wick
Photography:
Coco Amardei (2004)

Left: *Dancing Skeleton* paper
– protyped at Omni Colour then
printed water-based silk-screen

Above: *Electric Storm* mural with
Francis, King's Cross
Photography: Coco Amardeil
(2003)

Top right: *Reindeer Bone* wallpaper
at Mulberry, Bond Street, London
Photography: Jan Von Holleben
(2004)

Right: Abigail with *Volcanic
Eruption* mural and Skeleton tiled
fireplace, King's Cross
Photography: Coco Amardeil
(2003)

What do you aim to create with your work?
Small worlds into which I and others can submerge themselves
– if they please and while they last.

What inspired you to work with wallpaper? What is it that you like about this medium?
I always liked the fact that it enveloped you in a room – it is a good alternative to making the mental leap into the frame of a picture. Like Alice in Wonderland, you're through the looking glass and in the story.

Are there certain things you consider when designing a paper?
I have made wallpapers for museum and gallery exhibition as well as for homes. There is a difference between those made for people's private lives and those made for a museum audience. Although in some people's opinions the 'skeleton' print is macabre, it is still very playful and I believe it can work in many people's environments.

What do you always notice or look for when you enter a space?
A good-looking bloke – the bar – the door – not sure really, I suppose I look to see if it is the reflection of anybody interesting …

The whole room, or feature walls?
I think it often works well just to have 'feature walls'. It depends on the pattern; sometimes a whole room is just too much. I have one wall of our black skeleton print in my house – it's enough. I also like it when pictures are hung over the top and when the image is cut carefully around light sockets, doors and windows. The disruption almost reaffirms the power of the pattern as it reappears around the other side.

Answered by Abigail Lane

Left: *Reindeer Bone* paper
– protyped at Omni Colour then
printed Gravure in four special
colours

info@showroomdummies.com
www.showroomdummies.com
www.omnicolour.com

Francesco Simeti

Francesco Simeti was born in Palermo, Italy. He graduated in sculpture at the Art Academy in Bologna, Italy, and is currently working and living between Brooklyn and Sicily. He has created site-specific installations for Cooper Hewitt, National Museum of Design, New York; Wave Hill Glyndor Gallery, Bronx NY; Art & Idea Gallery, Mexico City and Columbia University, New York. His work has been exhibited among others at the Galleria d'Arte Moderna, Bologna, the Mu.dac, Musée de Design et d'Arts Appliqués Contemporains, Lausanne and the Institute of Contemporary Art, Philadelphia. He is represented by Galleria Francesca Minini in Milano.

'*Arabian Nights* (2003) was made for the Rhode Island School of Design Museum and is based on a chinoiserie paper belonging to the museum's collection. The pictures inserted are of post-"liberation" Afghanistan.'

Opposite: *Arabian Nights*
Above: *Arabian Nights*
installation, RISD Museum,
Providence, Rhode Island,
USA (2003)

'*Watching the War* (2002), a site-specific wallpaper for the Galleria d'Arte Moderna in Bologna, is made up of images of the American bombardment in Afghanistan.'

What would you say are the main influences on your work or style? Where do you draw inspiration?
The single most inspiring work is *Tutto* (Everything) by Alighiero e Boetti, which was the artist's attempt at encompassing the whole reality within one single tapestry.

Artists/designers/people you admire most?
I am interested in the work of Pino Pascali, Alighiero e Boetti, Oyvind Fahlstrom and the children's book illustrator Virginia Lee Burton.

What turns you on as an artist? What do you really like?
Hans Schabus's mountain installation at the 2005 Venice Biennale.

What do you aim to create with your work?
Aestheticize, disguise, destabilize.

What inspired you to work with wallpaper? What is it you like about this medium?
It is the perfect grid to organize and make sense of my archives of media clippings and it allows me to create hidden narratives.

Are there certain things you consider when designing a paper?
Most of my papers are born as site-specific work created for a specific space. When they are not, the starting point is constituted by one or two found images that I am compelled to use.

What's your preferred method of production and materials?
All my papers are digitally printed by Berlintapete in Germany.

What do you dislike with a passion?
Fundamentalism in its broadest sense.

To repeat, or not repeat?
Repetition is like reiteration, which is a fundamental conceptual aspect of my work.

For you, is wallpaper art or décor, or both?
Good wallpaper is Art, bad wallpaper is bad décor.

Opposite: *Watching the War*
Above: *Watching the War*
installation, Villa delle Rose,
Bologna, Italy (2002)

Opposite: *Crap on Crops*
Above: *Hawkes and Caves*
installation, Milan, Italy

In *Crap on Crops (2005)* pictures of planes crop dusting are superimposed over a rural landscape pattern reconstructed from a found wallpaper fragment.

Hawks and Caves (2004) was originally designed for Futura Gallery in Prague. The drawing of a cave, taken from a scholastic dictionary, is paired to a picture of American Black Hawk helicopters and a garland/vine design. The pattern was later used to wrap the scaffolding during the restoration of one of the historic gates of the city of Milan.

fsimeti@yahoo.com
www.francescaminini.it

Angel Souto

Spanish digital artist and designer Angel Souto fuses 3D images with 2D design creating info-graphic artworks. In 1998 he started work as a graphic designer and later took a masters degree in communication and digital creation. As one of Spain's leading graphic designers, his clients include Ericsson, Toyota, Inditex, E-innova and Telefónica. He has worked previously as an art director at Infarq and Urbansimulations and his design work has appeared in a number of leading publications including Web Design Index, Masters of Flash and Pink Project. He is the creator of the acclaimed site Atmosphere (www.zession. com/atmosphere) – a platform to show his work and more experimental designs.

What would you say are the main influences on your work or style? Where do you draw inspiration?
My influences are antiques, Japanese illustrations, painters – Feito, Tàpies, Chillida, Dali etc., and designers – Inocuo, Mike Young, Joshua Davis …

What turns you on as an artist? What do you really like?
The satisfaction of creating beautiful things.

What do you aim to create with your work?
To create sensations.

Are there certain things you consider when designing a paper?
The size, thin lines and the type size.

What's your preferred method of production and materials?
I like experimenting with different methods and materials; it's the best way to learn.

What do you always notice or look for when you enter a space?
Architecture, design, lights and the ambient space in general.

What do you dislike with a passion?
The disorder, the chaos.

The whole room, or feature walls?
Mmm, it depends, but if I have to choose … feature walls.

For you, is wallpaper art or décor, or both?
For me, wallpaper that produces sensations with cool work is art.

Favourite music to design/work with?
Sumo, Manu Chao, Extremoduro, Led Zeppelin, Nonpalidece, O Jarbanzo Negro, Pink Floyd, Björk, Mazzy Star, Vincent Gallo, Barrington Levy, African Messengers, Radio Futura, Tortoise, Ben Harper, Jack Johnson, Los Ronaldos etc …

Above: *MWP is YWP* (2005)

'This 3 x 6 m wallpaper *MWP is YWP* was made for the Maxalot
Gallery in Barcelona and I designed it as if it was for me.
The wallpaper takes a part of me, for that reason "My wallpaper
is your wallpaper."'

info@zession.com
www.zession.com
www.maxalot.com

Lisa Stickley

Lisa Stickley graduated in 2002 with an MA in printed textiles from the Royal College of Art, London. Since then she has worked on a variety of projects and commissions, including producing exclusive ranges of tableware for Burberry and Harrods. Lisa's signature is a combination of naïve imagery and interesting graphics that are quirky and very English. Lisa has been producing handmade textiles since she graduated, and Lisa Stickley London was set up in the summer 2003. More recent projects include a commission from Belmacz Ltd – making hand-printed felt packaging for their beautiful, contemporary jewellery collections. The *Shortbread* collection was launched in January 2005 in Le Bon Marché, Paris. Tablecloths from the *Notepaper* collection are now available at Selfridges & Co., London; and cushions from the *Mrs Perkins* collection are now available from Heals, London. She has exhibited in Milan, Japan, the Applied Arts Agency and the Crafts Council, London.

'My work is a personal interpretation and reinvention of the English tea room. *The Blackboard Wallpaper* collection stems from the *Notepaper* collection: an eclectic mix of printed notepaper, dots, flowers and menus, with a twist on 1950s-style domestic decoration. Inspiration for the Blackboard wallpaper is taken from many a traditional English café featuring the "menu of the day"'.

Where do you live and create your work?
In my studio, the Ivy House, in South London; I live in Clapham above an organic bakery.

What turns you on as an artist? What do you really like?
Eclectic objects with character, something that has been somewhere, loved, discarded and found again. Pieces like this have a loveliness of time that cannot be created in an instant.

Are there certain things you consider when designing a paper?
I prefer to consider composition for a single drop of wallpaper or a series of drops, single pieces rather than designs in repeat. It is nice to think each piece is completely individual.

What's your preferred method of production and materials?
Hand-printed, beautiful quality paper.

What do you always notice or look for when you enter a space?
Light and height.

What do you most dislike?
Lack of originality in design.

What's the future of wallpaper? How do you see it evolving?
Towards more conversational/interactive prints, also back to traditional papering used in a contemporary way – miss the walls, and use the ceiling and doors.

How would you like your own work to develop?
I would love time to focus on my wallpaper combined with my textiles and create a series of wall pieces, a handmade story for the wall.

Favourite music to design/work with?
Nina Simone.

Left: *Blackboard Rose and Menu and Blackboard Bouquet and Menu* (2004)

Opposite: *Blackboard Bouquet and Menu* (2004)

lisa@lisastickleylondon.com
www.lisastickleylondon.com

Oysters on toast
(Huitres sur canapés.)

Pompadour sandwiches.

rice and apple soufflé
(soufflé de Riz aux pommes)

Studio Job

Belgian designer Job Smeets established Studio Job in 1998 and was joined by Dutch born Nynke Tynagel in 2000. Both studied at the Design Academy Eindhoven (3D design and graphic design) and moved to Belgium in part to avoid being perceived as one of the Droog generation of Dutch designers. Their idiosyncratic style balances between art and design, creating furniture, interiors (wall coverings, tiles and fabrics), fashion, jewellery, industrial products, installations and objects for public space. 'Our design is about freedom. We think that design is a universal language spoken with shapes instead of words. In our design the important interaction is between onlooker and object. By looking at our objects, the onlooker looks directly into our eyes. In this sense our work is like a diary. Very intuitive and direct, we try to translate our experiences and ideas into an object or a collection.'

'We find the 2D surface a very demanding and not easy to satisfy area. A canvas or a wall is an empty space without anything to do: sometimes even without practical meaning. Because blank surfaces are so abstract, we sometimes cover them with signs. Skeletons, car wrecks, Etruscan signs, piercing eyes, prison bars or just pierrot-clowns ... anything can work as long as you know the right signs at the right moment!'

Opposite top: *Viking Blood Stain Room* (2004)
Opposite bottom: *Viking Boat Room* (2004)
Vikingen! exhibition, Centraal Museum
Utrecht, Netherlands

Left: *Viking Blood Pattern* (2004)

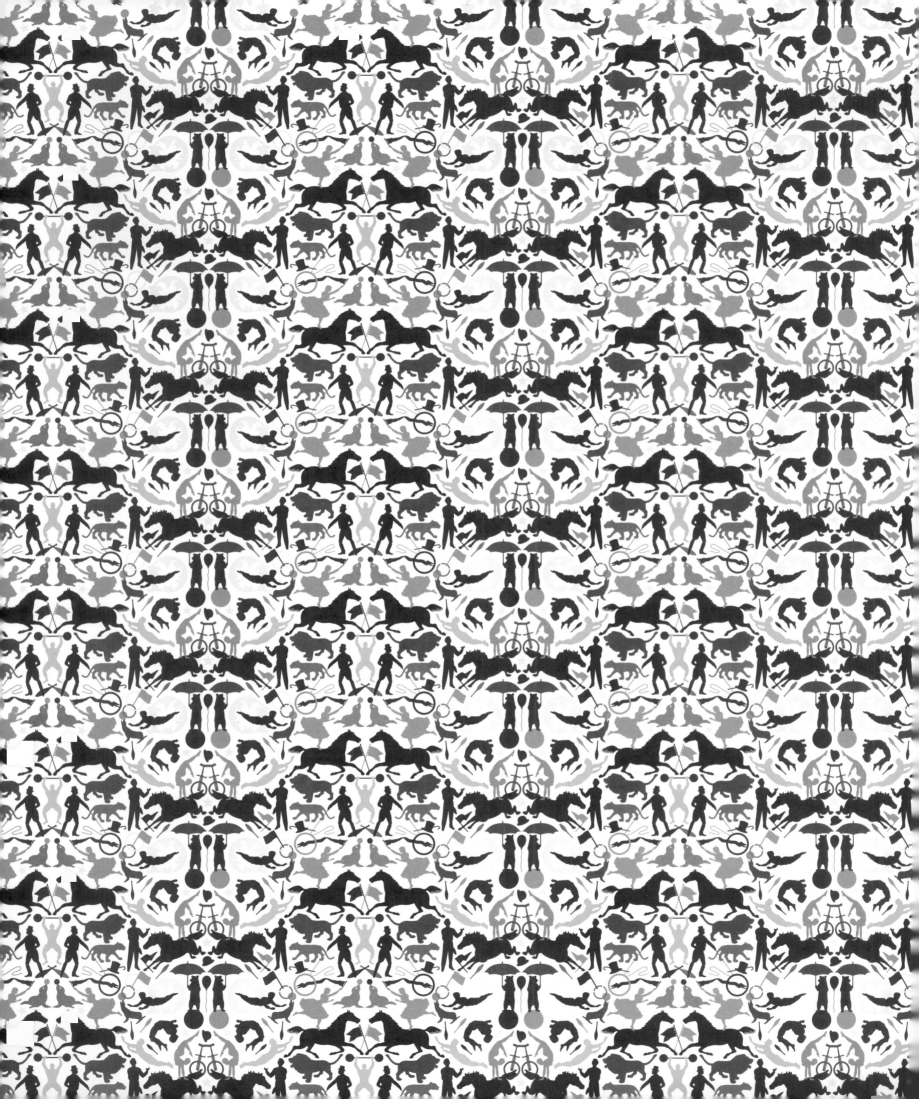

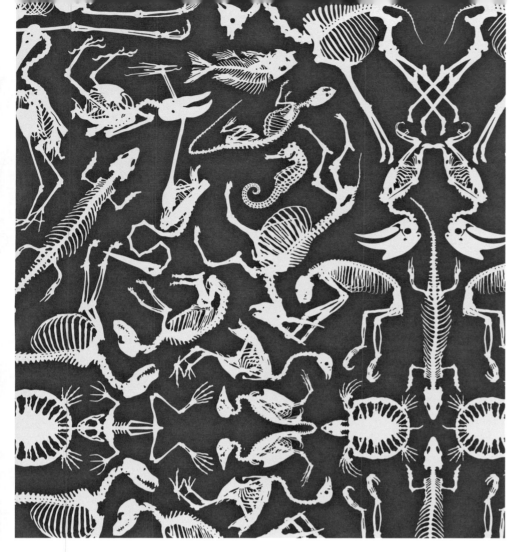

Artists/designers/people you admire most?
Today we love the work of the Flemish primitives (fourteenth century).

What inspired you to work with wallpaper? What is it you like about this medium?
You can create any illusion. It communicates very, very well.

Are there certain things you consider when designing a paper?
No, not even that we might use it for wallpaper. We just design compositions. And patterns with no real purpose … it's all very intuitive.

What's your preferred method of production and materials?
Mostly it's printed or pushed in relief. In the end we don't care about production. Or methods as long as our design is clear … that's the only thing that counts for us.

Do you have an ideal dream project? What would you most like to do?
Make huge paintings.

What do you dislike with a passion?
Hurting animals.

Less is more? Or blast the place with colour and pattern?
Fuck less is more … we think graphics are always very minimal.

How would you like your own work to develop?
Like an explosion, any direction!

Favourite music to design/work with?
At this moment the cello concerts by Bach played by Pablo Casals in 1936. The first recorded cello concerts … very special to hear the past.

Opposite: *Circus Pattern*
Top: *Skeleton Pattern*
Above: *Circus Pattern* gallery installation, Rotterdam, Netherlands (2004)

www.studiojob.be

Sweden Graphics

Nille Svensson graduated from Konstfack University College of Arts Crafts and Design in 1997. He founded Sweden Graphics together with Magnus Åström and has worked with design and illustration ever since.

Artists/designers/people you admire most?
Limiting myself to the design community, I think I envy more than I admire. It is not so much the quality of someone's work, but how they work and in what kind of position and creative conditions they have managed to put themselves. The more they have succeeded in synchronizing their talents with their output, the more admiration they get from me.

What turns you on as an artist? What do you really like?
Anything that is better than it has to be. Anything that reveals that there is a person behind the work that just couldn't let go until he or she was satisfied. It could be a multimillion-dollar commercial or a fanzine – that special nervous ambition always shines through.

What inspired you to work with wallpaper? What is it you like about this medium?
The nicest thing is that you can blend the content with the surface. Wallpapers are so common as a design medium that their presence is very unassuming and unpretentious: a fact that can be used to effect when adding content and communicative qualities to the design.

What do you always notice or look for when you enter a space?
If there is anyone in there that I know.

What do you dislike with a passion?
The feeling that there is not enough time.

The whole room, or feature walls?
Oh, I DO hate feature walls, or dekorväggar as they are called in Swedish. They're for cowards and are always the proof of total lack of taste.

What's the future of wallpaper? How do you see it evolving?
Wallpaper is perhaps like the suit in men's fashion, a hopelessly archaic phenomenon that somehow clings on in the lack of anything to take its place. The idea of gluing paper to the wall is a bit like having wooden floors in your car. On the other hand, there is a lot happening in paper-and-ink-based electronics. Perhaps future homes will have a lot of electronics integrated in the wallpaper. There are already wallpapers that can change their patterns to some extent.

How would you like your own work to develop?
More daring, more integrity, less compromise.

Favourite music to design/work with?
I've always wanted my design to be like the beginning of Phil Collins 'Susudio'. Quality beyond doubt.

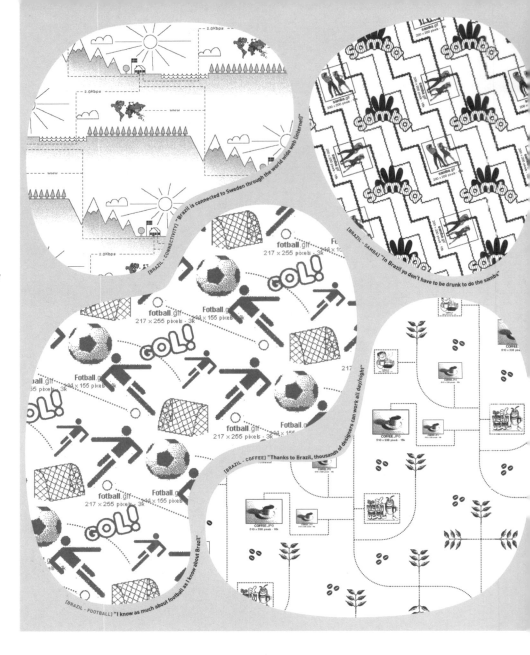

Opposite and above: *Brazil*

'The *Brazil* wallpaper patterns were designed for a book project initiated by Nando Costa. The idea was to gather different designers' expressions of how they were influenced by Brazil. I felt that my thoughts on Brazil were not very interesting or profound in themselves so I tried to turn the illustrations into something that would be interesting on a more aesthetic level.'

Photography: Ake E:son Lindman.
Architecture: Tham & Videgard Hansson

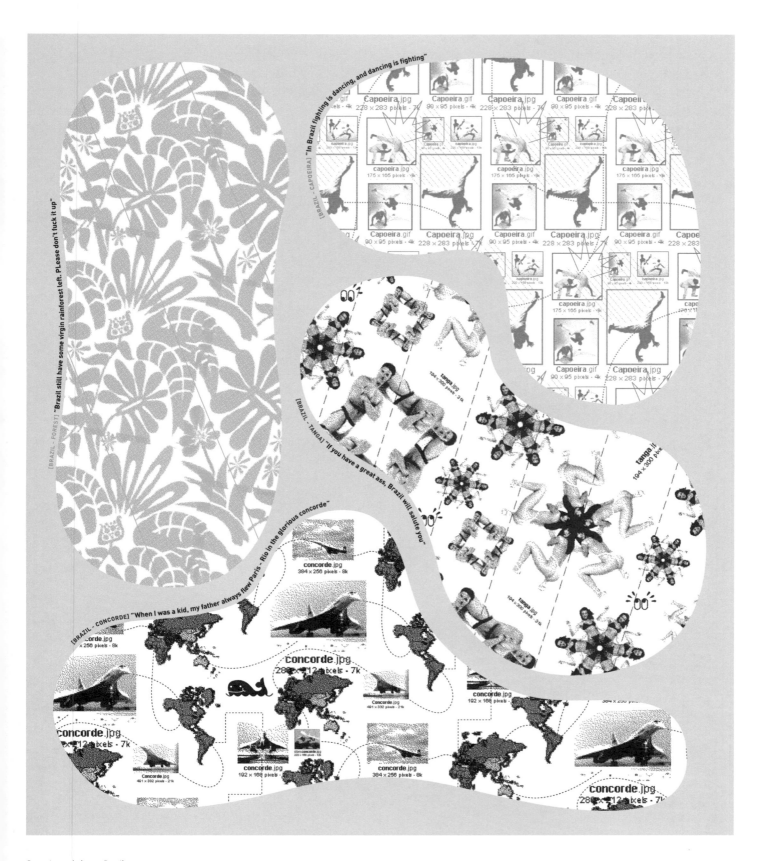

Opposite and above: *Brazil*
Photography: Ake E:son Lindman.
Architecture: Tham & Videgard Hansson

hello@swedengraphics
www.swedengraphics.com

Above: *Flow*, Exposif wallpapers, Maxalot

'*Flow* is a piece primarily about exploring space and movement. I wanted to create something like rolling hills or waves and winds that could take you and lose your self somewhere as your eyes work across the surface.'

Kam Tang

Kam Tang is a graphic designer and illustrator who lives and works in Brixton, London. Kam has continued to work as a freelance creative after studying graphic design at Brighton University and a masters at the Royal College of Art, London. He has designed work for many editorial publications, identities, advertising and music campaigns including *Wallpaper**, London's Design Museum and the Chemical Brothers, as well as his own solo shows in Japan. Kam continues to work in a variety of media and styles, and looks forward to the next project to develop his own unique visual language.

Artists/designers/people you admire most?
Pushpin Studios and Jack Kirby are two I hold in high regard.

What turns you on as an artist? What do you really like?
New stuff I've not seen before; people who plough their own furrow.

What do you aim to create with your work?
A communication of ideas, aesthetics and personal gratification.

What inspired you to work with wallpaper? What is it you like about this medium?
I was asked, but I have been itching to work on a larger scale for some time after working on smaller scale mediums such as CDs. Obviously size and the aspect of environment, that it's an immersive experience. The idea of walking into a piece as opposed to turning a page or picking something up is very appealing.

Are there certain things you consider when designing a paper?
The scale, the impact, the way the onlooker will perceive the work and becomes part of the work as they walk into it and whether or not it should repeat.

Preferred method of production and materials?
Drawing with pen and paper followed by Mac.

What do you always notice or look for when you enter a space?
The size, atmosphere, the contents and the exit.

What do you dislike with a passion?
Chelsea Football Club.

Favourite music to design/work with?
Usually Mozart or Radio 4 but it generally depends on my mood. Coltrane is good when the going gets heavy.

mail@kamtang.com
www.kamtang.com
www.maxalot.com

Timorous Beasties

Timorous Beasties is a design-led manufacturing company based in Glasgow, Scotland, started by Paul Simmons and Alistair McAuley in the early 1990s. Specializing in fabrics and wallpapers, Timorous Beasties have worked on many large-scale site-specific projects for clients all over the world. Their early work has been described as 'William Morris on acid' and could be seen as a wayward take on the often 'twee' world of textiles, with heavily illustrative insects, triffid-like plants and large-scale fish swirling in intricate patterns and repeats that adorn rich and heavy fabrics. Their more recent work is as graphic and modern as it is varied.

'The *Damask Circle* wallpaper is a traditional damask image that has been overprinted with opaque inks in concentric circles, so that both designs, old and new, compete with each other in the overall pattern.

The *London Toile* is a contemporary take on the old toiles that were produced in a pre-revolutionary and post-industrial France in the small town of Jouey in the 1770s. The urban landscape is changing all the time, modern buildings have become the new icons that give us a strong sense of identity; the *London Toile* is a perfect expression of this, talking to us in the present using the past.'

Artists / designers / people you admire most?
To name but a few, Dutch design, Josef Frank, William Morris, Joseph Beuys, Paul Klee, Leonardo da Vinci, Picasso, Ridley Scott, Tom Kirk, Chuck Mitchell, Italian motorcycles, Quasimoto, the Chapman Brothers, Ricky Gervais, Mona Hatoum and so on …

What turns you on as an artist? What do you really like?
Art, food, ancient history, ornithology and hip-hop.

What inspired you to work with wallpaper? What is it you like about this medium?
Initially it was a cost effective way of producing some of our designs for people to see.

Opposite: *Damask Circle*
Left: *London Toile*

'The *Oriental Orchid* design shows delicate orchids intertwining with the slightly darker side of life. The organic shapes of the orchids are combined with the graphic of a Manga cartoon to expose the sexual nature of the flowers. The overlays of matte and gloss inks, and the subtlety of the graphic print over the organic forms, demonstrate the unique qualities that can be produced through hand-printing.'

Are there certain things you consider when designing a paper?
Yes, lots, for example, whether the wallpaper has balance and repeats well, using inks for layering colours or glossy inks for different effects, or opaque inks to retain bright colours when overlapped.

What's your preferred method of production and materials?
Hand-print, you can't beat a hand-print quality.

Do you have an ideal dream project? What would you most like to do?
Wallpaper a tower block.

What do you dislike with a passion?
Artex, it will never look good. Carpets in toilets.

To repeat, or not repeat?
Depends, oh I don't know, depends, oh I don't know, depends ...

For you, is wallpaper art or décor, or both?
Décor, we're not artists we're designers.

What's the future of wallpaper? How do you see it evolving?
Yes, it will change, digital will bring in a lot more scale, and bespoke, and then we will go back to minimalism, then back to decoration then back to ... like a big repeat into infinity!

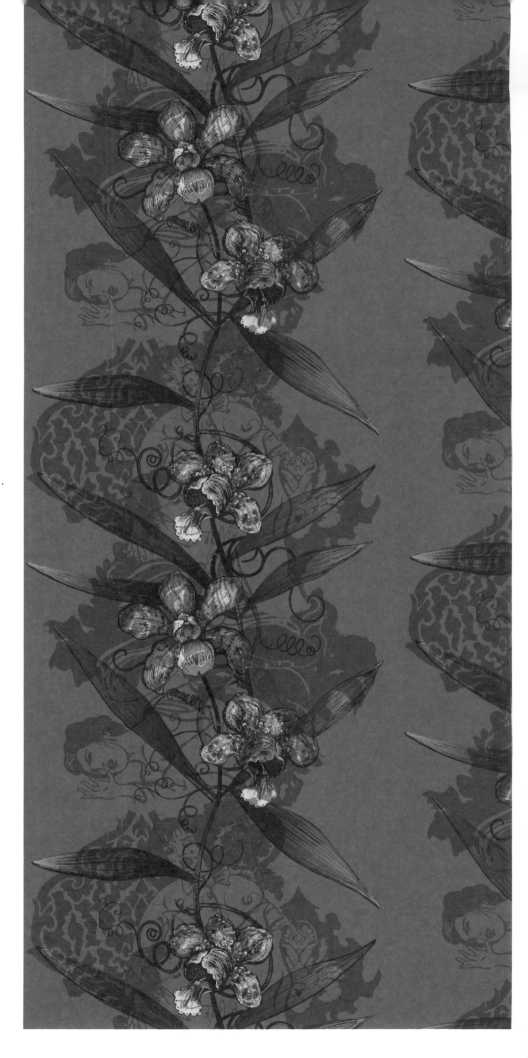

info@timorousbeasties.com
www.timorousbeasties.com

Opposite and right:
Oriental Orchid wallpaper

Above: *Urban Wallpaper*

'*Urban Wallpaper* is a set of three sheets of 'lambe-lambe' poster that must be applied side by side just as wallpaper would. The 'lambe-lambe' technique (printing, paper stock and application) is very popular in Brazil to promote shows and cultural events in public spaces due to its low cost. All of the inherent limitations of this process were incorporated in the design of what ultimately became a very personal piece. *Urban Wallpaper* was featured at the second Resfest Brazil as part of the special design projects sponsored by the festival. It was showcased at the MASP (São Paulo Museum of Art) metro station's exit corridors for the duration of the festival.'

Clarissa Tossin

A graduate from FAAP in São Paulo, Brazil, Clarissa Tossin is a visual artist who mainly explores the venues of graphic design and illustration. She experienced her first major breakthrough by winning the prestigious gold award of the Brazilian design Biennial ADG. This in turn led her to start her own 'one woman' design studio: A'. In a matter of months, Clarissa emerged on both the Brazilian and international scene with shows in Paris, Vienna and Toronto; and work published in magazines and books around the world. Her clients have included such household names as: Vogue, MTV, Nike, Dupont, O2 Filmes and local icons such as Hotel Fasano and São Paulo Fashion Week. She met Jonathan Notaro – owner of Brand New School – who on seeing her work immediately offered her a full-time position at his Santa Monica studio. Clarissa accepted the offer and moved to the US where she currently resides and works.

Artists/designers/people you admire most?
Lucio Costa and Oscar Niemeyer for their visionary ideas embodied in the city of Brasilia. John Warwicker for his attitude and body of work. John Maeda, Clarice Lispector and many other artists that showed me things that I had never been able to perceive before coming into contact with their work.

Was there a defining moment when you decided to become a designer?
I consider myself a visual artist who explores the venues of graphic design and illustration. These two areas alone offer a wide range of different possibilities. However, I am always open to experimental projects beyond these self-defined boundaries.

What turns you on as an artist? What do you really like?
I like to see my work as part of the visual production that permeates people's daily lives. I share an interest in both solid conceptual visual projects and eye-catching formal driven ones. My degree in graphic design in conjunction with my work as an image maker enables me to appreciate both ends of the spectrum. I am also drawn to inter-disciplinary projects that combine graphic design with fashion, architecture, cinema, art and music to further an idea.

What do you aim to create with your work?
Communication. Reaction. Dialogue.

What inspired you to work with wallpaper? What is it you like about this medium?
The interaction with the urban geography. The people flow as a starting point for the interaction with the visual piece.

ola@a-linha.org
www.a-linha.org

Hanna Werning

Hanna Werning studied graphic design at Central Saint Martins College of Art & Design in London. Returning to Sweden in 2004, Hanna settled in Stockholm where she founded her own studio specializing in pattern, art and design. Her work could be defined in two categories; one where the design is driven by an idea or a concept, and the other where the image is driven by intuition and colour rhythm. In London, Hanna was employed as a senior designer at Foundation 33, working on projects for Channel 4, Island Records and MTV etc. She has also been designing textile patterns for Borås Cotton (SE), the bag company Eastpak and fashion labels including Boxfresh (UK), Stüssy (USA) and Dagmar (SE). In 2004, she received the Swedish *Elle Decoration* Design Award (EDIDA) for 'Wall-coverings and Wallpaper'.

Hanna (wallpaper collection) was launched in 2006 in collaboration with the Swedish wallpaper manufacturer Boråstapeter. Six wallpaper patterns were designed and produced in 2005 – *Näckrosryss, Svanpark, Nötplockare, Kvitter, Katträd* and *Kastanjetrast.*

Left: *Katträd*
Repeat size: 53 x 53 (half repeat)
Photography: Dan Holmqvis
Styling: Gabriella Heintz

Overleaf: *Kastanjetrast, Kvitter*

AnimalFlowers (wallpaper-posters 2001–4) is a collection of seven patterns entitled *Krokodillöv, Flodhästvår, Sjöhästäng, Ekorreblad, Djurträdgård, Zebraskog* and *Elefantgräs*. All are based on the themes of animal silhouettes and floral shapes, and include multi-coloured collages of old and new ornaments. The first sketches were drawn during Hanna's last year at Central Saint Martins in 2001. Her best-known designs are made to work as a single poster as well as wallpaper. The idea is that you buy as many poster-sheets as you need to cover a certain area or just one for framing.

What would you say are the main influences on your work or style? Where do you draw inspiration?
From my childhood, John Bauer, 1970s comics, the woods and my mum's old wardrobe. Normally I just get hooked on something and get an idea that I would like to complete. If I have a brief I collect readings on the theme, then I highlight words that I later look up in a thesaurus. These words normally give me a starting point for a concept. For a pattern I work more visually from the beginning. I wonder around in buildings, at art exhibitions, in the streets, in parks and take lots of pictures of interesting details, look at antique books and clouds.

Artists/designers/people you admire most?
Peggy Guggenheim, Meret Oppenheim, Bridget Riley, Saul Bass, Frida Kahlo, Charles and Ray Eames, Carl Johan de Geer, James Turrell, Hektor, Olafur Eliasson.

Are there certain things you consider when designing a paper?
I'm trying to be as intuitive as possible while creating patterns. I think more of the rhythm of the repeat, the number of colours and different layers, rather than what motifs I choose to include into the design. I am not trying to make a story or a collage of ornaments that makes sense. That is up to the viewer to create.

The whole room, or feature walls?
Feature walls. Or rather, feature objects – wrap up an old drawer or electricity locker in an odd paper.

How would you like your own work to develop?
Create more conceptual pieces such as my *Apparat No.1* where the pattern design is derived by a system. I like the surprise moment in design. When an accident happens and it turns out in a way I never imagined – something that my hand would never be able to create.

Opposite and above: *Krokodillöv, AnimalFlowers* wallpaper-posters (2001–4) Repeat size: 50 x 70
Print: Litho. on 115 gsm paper

Left: *Flodhästvår*

www.byhanna.com

Opposite: *Pineapple*
Above: *Gerbera*

Jenny Wilkinson

Jenny Wilkinson is an independent designer who grew up in Paris and London before studying design at Chelsea College, London and later 3D design for production at Brighton University. She set up her design studio in 2003 and currently designs and manufactures her own range of wallpapers, which are distributed in the UK, Europe and across the US. Alongside designing and manufacturing her own range of products, Jenny also undertakes individual commissions and contract work. She has more recently been working on numerous projects with the US company 2 Jane. Her portfolio of work also includes surface design in wood, metal, ceramics and plastics.

What would you say are the main influences on your work or style? Where do you draw inspiration?
At the moment I am inspired by all sorts of graphic design and illustration, I am a bit like a magpie and pick up on anything that catches my eye, from graphics in magazines to flyers and street art.

Artists/designers/people you admire most?
Just a few of the people I admire are: Hayao Miyazaki, Marcel Wanders, Banksy, Rousseau, Timorous Beasties, Ron Arad, Nick Crosbie (Inflate), Verner Panton, Quentin Blake and Tord Boontje.

What turns you on as an artist? What do you really like?
I really like fun. I love the element of fun and playfulness in design, I love a good idea. I love work that brings a smile to my face, bright and bold colours, print and patterns.

Are there certain things you consider when designing a paper?
With the *Wallpaper-By-Numbers* prints I have to consider how it will look as a painted print as well as an outline pattern. Some designs I have worked with have looked great as a full-colour painted print, but then looked awful as an outline print or vice versa, which can be quite frustrating at times.

What do you always notice or look for when you enter a space?
Pattern and shapes. I am always looking for interesting repeats, whether it be wallpaper, textile or objects. For example, waiting for my bag to arrive in baggage reclaim at Heathrow airport I found myself seeing a great repeat where all the trolleys were stacked up!

What's the future of wallpaper? How do you see it evolving?
It is a medium that is being given a new lease of life, anything goes! What I have found most exciting is that it has become cross-disciplinary. Fashion designers, graphic designers, product designers, illustrators, so many people are turning their hand to wallpaper and the results and interpretations are all so different. Also, new manufacturing capabilities for wallpaper are opening up a whole new avenue for exploring and pushing ideas.

'*Wallpaper-By-Numbers* is a new idea in interactive wallpaper. It takes its inspiration from the 1950s craze of paint-by-numbers; by increasing the size of the print from a canvas to a whole wall, the user has to make a decision on where they are going to start painting and how much they are going to paint, in doing so, personalizing their walls (be it one repeat, a diagonal stripe, a border or picture-sized square).'

jenny@paint-by-numbers.co.uk
www.paint-by-numbers.co.uk

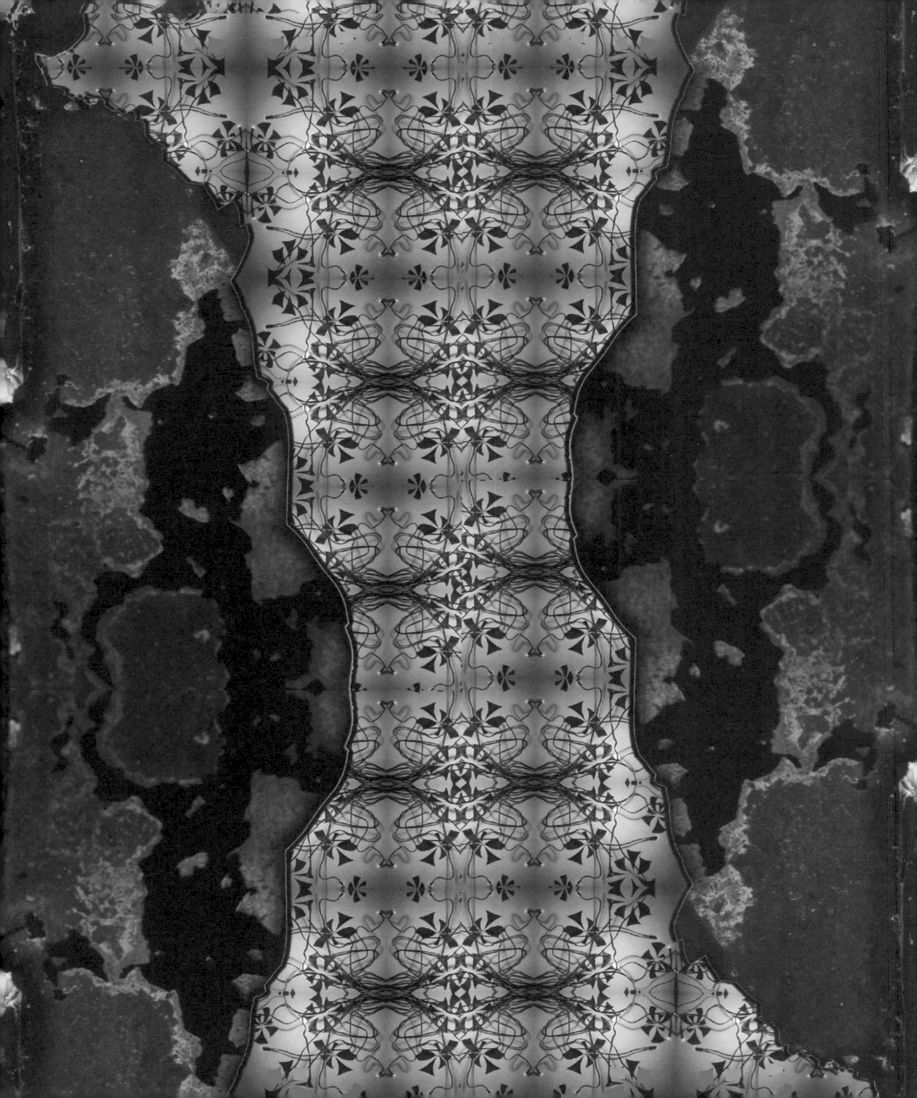

Maria Yaschuk

Maria Yaschuk was born in Moscow but spent her teenage years in Norway before moving to London to study art. During the first year of foundation she fell in love with London and decided to continue her design studies at the London College of Printing with a BA in print media – surface design. During the course she engaged a diverse range of surface design applications (mainly screen-printing) in textiles, ceramics, paper, board and plastics. Then at Central Saint Martins College of Art & Design (MA design for textile futures) her personal project investigated the use of interactive, experiential design, ambient computing and interface design within home interiors – attempting to challenge the nature of surface and textile design through the use of interactive technologies. This project led to a big commission for a variety of wallpapers that were placed in an office in the Canary Wharf area (ADP Wilco Ltd, The ISIS Building, 193 Marsh Wall, London).

'The world around us is a beautiful and fascinating pattern of chaos and ordered complexity. I am captivated by its mysterious structure and the way we create and incorporate our structures within it. *Wire Geometrics* is the collection that explores the connection and interdependence of real physical space and the virtual space created by the surrounding environment. Through playing with light patterns and integrating lighting technologies into wallpaper I am trying to construct a powerful, majestic and futuristic atmosphere in the interior.'

Opposite, above and right:
Wire Geometrics – Light Mysteries
collection (2004)

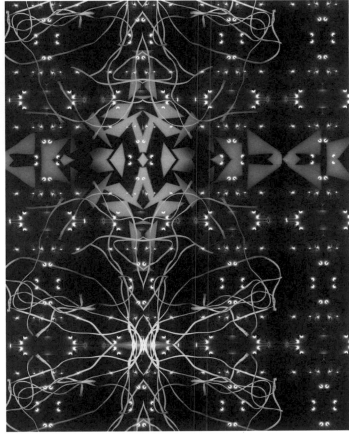

Where do you draw inspiration?
The main inspiration is the experience of the space and environments around me, from small details in nature to the city landscape, dreams and fantasy worlds.

Artists/designers/people you admire most?
Yayoi Kusama for creating spaces from patterns, Fabio Novembre for freedom of shape and expression, Ingo Maurer for the delicacy of line and object.

What turns you on as an artist? What do you really like?
New experiences, mysteries, scientific discoveries, other dimensions, nature's chaos and the self-similarity of forms and textures.

What do you always notice or look for when you enter a space?
Usually when I enter the space I don't look for anything in particular … I rather let the space 'talk' to me. All places and spaces are different but harmony within the space is something I really love.

What's the future of wallpaper? How do you see it evolving?
Keep the wall, evolve the paper.

Favourite music to design/work with?
No music. Music is a very influential medium. It changes my mood and thought; I get carried away with it. When I work I get carried away with the pattern of shapes and colours that create 'music' as they develop …

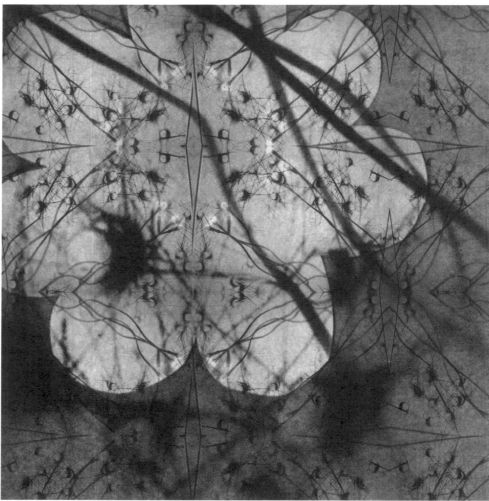

Above and opposite bottom:
Flower Photo – Light Mysteries collection (2004)

Opposite top:
LED Light – Wire Geometrics
– Light Mysteries collection (2004)
Digital print that incorporates 93 real LED lights

maria_yaschuk@yahoo.com

Peter Zuiderwijk

Peter Zuiderwijk has been working as an independent graphic designer since 1999 after graduating from the Royal Academy in The Hague, the Netherlands. Next to commissioned work that includes clients such as the Dutch Council of Culture and the Dutch National Aviation Theme Park, Aviodrome, Zuiderwijk participates in the artist-platform <>TAG with the magazine *TAGMAG* and initiates semi-independent projects with his partner Karin Mientjes. Since 2002 Zuiderwijk has been teaching image development in editorial design at the Willem de Kooning Academy in Rotterdam and has been a visiting member of faculty at the Maryland Institute College of Art, Baltimore, USA.

What's your preferred method of production and materials?
The actual production was based upon Maxalot's large format printing philosophy. The use of a printer makes production flexible, the design can be customized. We are no longer limited by printing techniques or format issues, the only limitations are architectural and physical, and of course aesthetical. In a sense, there is no longer a need to repeat patterns; the innovations on a production level are almost unlimited. A deeper question is: 'How can you perceive without thinking in clichés?' We are numbed and brainwashed by visual imagery, and in this respect wallpaper is a perfect metaphor: we live in an overkill of repeating images.

What do you always notice or look for when you enter a space?
Details; how stuff is organized, how specified and how standardized a space is (think doors, light switches, handles, ceilings etc.). Boring stuff can be so inspirational.

What's the future of wallpaper? How do you see it evolving?
I love all those stories about nano technology and what you could do with it. The thought that you can buy television per litre and paint it on every possible surface. Every surface can be used as television, wallpaper or graffiti. What will this mean for designers and, very important, hackers?

How would you like your own work to develop?
Less 'You ask and I make' and more 'I make and you ask'. Don't tell me what to do, but do trigger me and push my boundaries. Annoy me, I like it ...

'*Dutch Eldorado* is based on historical, technical and aesthetical research into wallpaper. Thematically, the design tries to translate historical facts into a contemporary design system. Looking at order versus chaos in Dutch society, the design focuses on places that seem to be overlooked by others due to lack of (human) order – like void spaces filled with all sorts of weeds. *Dutch Eldorado* deconstructs the Legoland-like Dutch infrastructure to its smallest details, juxtaposing it with the natural, seemingly chaotic, abundance. The Dutch have achieved the perfect order, yet they crave the excitement of the unknown.

'The design was built up out of three separate designs; the small strip on the outside was designed for close range, the medium strip for an average distance and the big strip in the middle for long distances. On another level you can link the same system to the history of wallpaper production. The separate designs relate to technical boundaries; the outside stripes relate to old-fashioned block print designs, while the centre piece relates to modern large format printing that knows no boundaries when it comes to the design.'

info@peterzuiderwijk.com
www.peterzuiderwijk.com
www.maxalot.com

Above: *Dutch Eldorado Wallpaper* at TAG Headquarters, The Hague

Opposite: *Dutch Eldorado Wallpaper* (2005) Exposif wallpapers, Maxalot

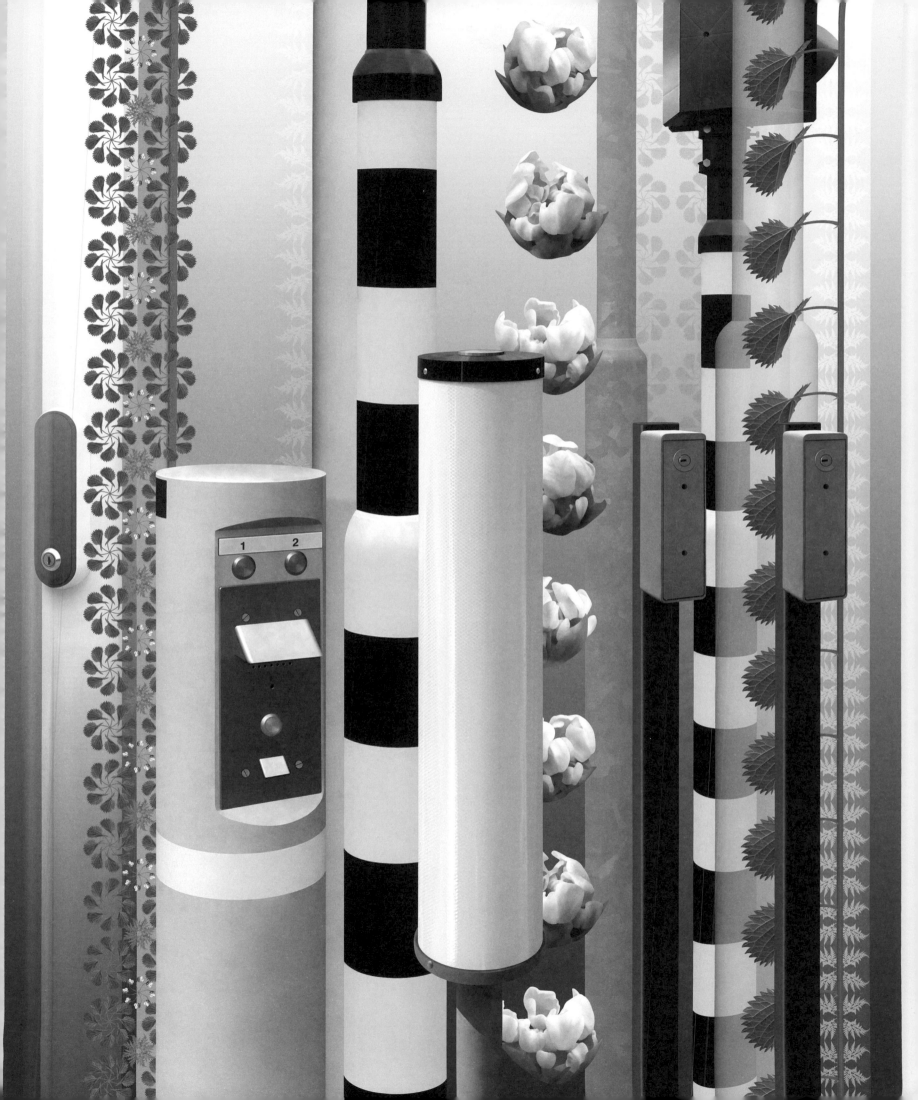